The Next Big Thing

A Rough Guide to things that seemed like a good idea at the time

D1355227

www.roughguides.com

Credits

The Next Big Thing

Edit, design and layout:
Andrew Clare
Proofreading: Susanne Hillen
Production: Rebecca Short

Rough Guides Reference

Director: Andrew Lockett
Editors: Kate Berens, Peter Buckley,
Tracy Hopkins, Matthew Milton,
Joe Staines, Ruth Tidball

Publishing information

This first edition published October 2009 by
Rough Guides Ltd, 80 Strand, London, WC2R 0RL
375 Hudson Street, NY 10014, USA
Email: mail@roughguides.com

Distributed by the Penguin Group:
Penguin Books Ltd, 80 Strand, London, WC2R 0RL
Penguin Group (USA), 375 Hudson Street, NY 10014, USA
Penguin Group (Australia), 250 Camberwell Road, Camberwell, Victoria 3124, Australia
Penguin Group (Canada), 90 Eglinton Avenue East, Suite 700, Toronto, Ontario, Canada M4P 2Y3
Penguin Group (New Zealand), Cnr Rosedale and Airborne Roads, Albany, Auckland, New Zealand

Printed and bound in Singapore

Typeset in Montara, Myriad and Minion

Front cover image courtesy of Corbis

216 pages; includes index

A catalogue record for this book is available from the British Library.

ISBN 13: 978-1-84836-352-6

1 3 5 7 9 8 6 4 2

The Next Big Thing

A Rough Guide to things that seemed like a good idea at the time

Rhodri Marsden

ROUGH GUIDES

www.roughguides.com

Contents

Introduction   7

1 **Posthumous libation and naked gyration:**
Ancient Egypt, Greece and Rome   11

2 **Self-inflicted welts and chastity belts:**
The Dark and Middle Ages   31

3 **Bleeding to death and malodorous breath:**
1450–1650   51

4 **Look at a freak, or play hide-and-seek:**
1650–1900   71

5 **Prohibiting booze, goldfish in the news:**
1900–1950   91

6 **Concrete blocks and minuscule frocks:**
The Fifties and Sixties   111

7 **Immobile pets and King Crimson cassettes:**
The Seventies 131

8 **Aerobic larks and abandoning Marx:**
The Eighties 151

9 **Sugary booze and Celtic tattoos:**
The Nineties 171

10 **Sudoku puzzling and Viagra guzzling:**
The 2000s 191

11 **But surely these can't last, either?**
The future 203

Index 211

Acknowledgements

Many thanks to Louisa Nicoll, Sam Gould, John Ellingsworth, Serena Cowdy, Leanne Rae Wierzba, Joanna Cordero, Alice Waugh, Rob Desjardins, Luke Pitcher, Justine Wolfenden, John Rooney, Abigail Balfe and Amanda Hawkins, all of whom helped to fill in yawning gaps in my historical knowledge by pitching in a range of fascinating and funny ideas. Thanks also to various Internet communities on Twitter, Facebook and LiveJournal, whose citizens inexplicably leapt to my aid with nuggets of information. Much gratitude to Elliot Elam for his wonderful sketches, and special thanks to Jenny McIvor for brutally red-penning my hackneyed observations and obtuse grammar. You all helped to make this book better.

Introduction

Thank goodness that common sense deserts us from time to time. Imagine how lacking in sparkle our everyday existences would be if we didn't occasionally make absurd decisions, such as jumping in a fountain fully clothed, belching loudly at a christening, writing a song about an errant tortoise or marrying our cousin. Without hare-brained, impetuous plans and preposterous ideas to add some va-va-voom to our waking hours, we would all proceed in a preordained, predictable fashion – in fact, our lives probably wouldn't be worth living at all. And after we'd all gone through the motions, history could be plotted on a gently sloping graph, free of kinks and looking for all the world like the performance data of a highly efficient combustion engine.

But sometimes we're liable to jump happily on a bandwagon and collectively decide that something is a great idea, while somehow

Introduction

managing to suppress any niggling thoughts in the back of our minds that it might all be a load of rubbish. We usually come to our senses after a while; we're able to look back with the benefit of hindsight and gasp at our naivety, lack of taste or downright stupidity, before immediately plunging ourselves into some new, ill-thought-out activity that will inevitably be judged by future generations as being a bit silly, too. We can't help ourselves. We're doomed to do it.

In 1974 and 1975, a colossal proportion of British teenage girls clad themselves in ankle-length tartan trousers and tartan scarves, and screamed at deafening volume at the Bay City Rollers, a band from Scotland who you could safely say weren't pushing back the frontiers of songwriting. But by the summer of 1977, you'd be hard pushed to find any girls who'd be prepared to admit that they'd ever had anything tartan lurking in their wardrobe. Total embarrassment and shame had descended. And if it wasn't for the video evidence, we wouldn't have known that it had happened at all. "Bye Bye Baby" is

no worse or better a record today than it was when it was released, but you don't find anyone wearing a tam-o'shanter and playing it over and over again while bawling loudly.

You see, humans are terribly fickle creatures; recipes that excite our taste buds today might revolt us by the following Tuesday, and ornaments that our grandparents once cherished are unceremoniously jettisoned into skips if they don't coincide with our current aesthetic outlook. We live our lives amid a complex web of rapidly changing whims, desires, ethics and policies; we pick the ones we like, and they form the spirit of our age, the spirit of our society. The *zeitgeist*. When we're bored with those, we quietly disown them and quickly find something else. And that becomes the new *zeitgeist*. But what we can't ever do is get rid of the *zeitgeist*. It's always knocking about.

What is it comprised of today? A zillion things: hatred of bankers; the word LOL; a bizarre love of competitive TV-based ballroom dancing; a disinterest in the plight of factory-farmed chickens; and

the Kings Of Leon. (See p.203 for a more exhaustive rundown.) In a hundred years' time, it might be uploading the contents of your brain to someone else's during the night as a joke so they wake up feeling all disorientated, zinc handbags, and cannibalism. We have no idea. But what we can do is look back over several millennia of history and laugh at, wince at or, very occasionally, rehabilitate things that our ancestors thought were completely brilliant, but then realized at some point weren't that good after all.

This book gently attempts to collect some of those things together into a whistle-stop cultural history. It mourns, celebrates and – more often – mocks the stuff that wasn't quite good enough to recommend to the next generation; we'll look at what some of these things were, why we thought they were amazing, and why, ultimately, we lost interest in them. Of course, we've had to impose a few limits: any antics that non-Western civilizations got up to in the past two or three thousand years are probably best left to another book (the West has made quite enough poor choices of its own) so if you're looking for the Zoroastrian habit of placing the dead on the top of a tall column to be devoured by vultures, I'm afraid you won't find it here (although you will find people at the top of long poles for quite different reasons – see p.96).

We've also tried to be sensitive towards innovators – people who came up with ideas that were undeniably great, but were simply superseded by a better piece of technology. For example, there's nothing inherently wrong with the 8-track cartridge; it didn't fall out of favour because we realized it was terrible. It just wasn't quite as convenient or cheap as the cassette. No, what we've been looking for are bizarre fads, dead-end trends, inexplicable beliefs – all demonstrating the ephemeral nature of our needs and aspirations. Eating swans. Tamagotchi. Crinolines. Ouija boards. The things that just make you think: WHY?

Posthumous libation and naked gyration:
Ancient Egypt, Greece and Rome

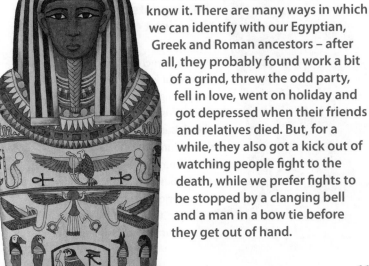

It's civilization, sure, but not as we know it. There are many ways in which we can identify with our Egyptian, Greek and Roman ancestors – after all, they probably found work a bit of a grind, threw the odd party, fell in love, went on holiday and got depressed when their friends and relatives died. But, for a while, they also got a kick out of watching people fight to the death, while we prefer fights to be stopped by a clanging bell and a man in a bow tie before they get out of hand.

We're happy to eat beans, because we don't imagine for a moment that they might contain the souls of the dead. We don't shave off our own arm hair unless we're very drunk. False beards are only worn for comedy purposes. Lettuce is consumed for its mild health benefits rather than for any massive increase in sexual potency. Togas have been assessed as too cumbersome and unwieldy. Didactic poetry isn't the publishing sensation it once was.

In short, we've changed. Hopefully for the better. But then again, the Egyptians, the Greeks and the Romans never had to cope with operating five separate remote control handsets in order to be entertained in their own homes. So maybe we're the misguided ones after all.

Putting cats on a pedestal they didn't particularly deserve

Cats don't generally show a great amount of interest in what we're doing, unless we're opening a can of delicious meaty chunks in close proximity to their empty food bowl. But their ability to rid the streets of vermin saw the Egyptians elevate the humble moggy to godlike status. If your own cat died, you'd enter a period of uncontrollable grief, get it mummified, and lop off your eyebrows as a mark of respect. If you were unfortunate enough to be found guilty of killing one, you'd be looking at the death penalty.

But the creation of the cat-goddess, Bast, along with the city of Bubastis and its adjoining temple – a veritable shrine to the grace and poise of the domestic feline – saw the Egyptian cat obsession get slightly out of proportion. In fact, it eventually led to their downfall; the cunning Persians, at the Battle of Pelusium in 525 BC, let cats loose on the battlefield while also having cat images emblazoned on their shields. The Egyptians didn't know where to look, or what to do. They were routed, and this defeat marked the end of the line of Pharaohs. Worth bearing in mind, if you ever consider building a shrine to little Speckles.

Women shaving their heads and then wearing wigs on top

Wigs are sported by very few people in the modern world: fashion models; men embarrassed at the rapid onset of baldness; people undergoing chemotherapy; and eccentric old ladies. They're all either slightly shamefaced about the fact that they're wearing them, or a little too eager to draw attention to the fact that they're wearing them.

But to Ancient Egyptians, the wig was pretty normal, and women vastly preferred its reliability and consistency to their own locks, which they'd simply shave off. Once they'd got rid of every last hair with gold tweezers, they'd buff their scalp with sand and pick out a wig made, ironically, from human hair (although cheaper wigs would be padded out with vegetable fibre). It's a brilliant idea that could do with being re-adopted across the world. No one would ever have a bad hair day. No one would get depressed about the inadequate follicles that had been genetically bequeathed to them by their parents. They'd just get rid of it all, and buy something that suited them. Keep it in a box, no shampoo necessary, and wake up to a nice, clean bald head every morning, rather than a greasy, lopsided mess. Why did we ever let this one go?

Wearing leopard skin to deliver religious sermons

Most Egyptians wore a simple, rectangular piece of linen to preserve their modesty. Priests generally kept things understated, too, and opted for plain fabric. However, the Sem priests – who performed the elaborate rituals associated with the burial of the dead – were permitted to jazz up the occasion with a sassy little leopard skin number. While there was ostensibly a good reason for this (the skin was associated with the God Seth, the adversary of mankind, and the wearing of it symbolized human triumph over him) you can't help but feel that the Sem priest revelled in his ability to slink around the temple like a prowling feline.

Today, of course, you'd only see a man of the cloth sporting leopard skin if he were delivering a risqué performance of a Tina Turner number at a charity karaoke event. And even then he probably wouldn't enjoy wearing it. The fact that leopard skin is now inappropriate at any church ceremony – let alone a funeral – is somehow testament to the decline in its religious importance.

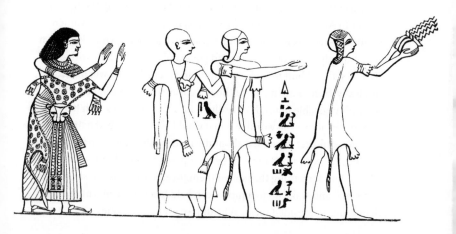

Preserving dead bodies with a spot of myrrh

Today, we're resigned to the idea that our deceased nearest and dearest will go through some kind of subterranean decomposition procedure – that is if they've not already been reduced to a pile of ash in a furnace. But in Ancient Egypt it was all about keeping their form as well preserved as possible in preparation for the afterlife. Of course, the quality of the procedure was largely down to how much money you had to spend, and it's likely that the "budget mummification" service consisted of little more than a quick evisceration and a wash and scrub before being handed back. But the top-of-the-range, gilt-edged service was magnificently detailed.

The organs would be removed and placed in Canopic jars – except for the brain, which would be dragged through the nostrils with hooks and quietly disposed of. The inner cavity of the body would be treated with palm wine, myrrh and spices such as cassia, before being sewn up and smeared with natron, a salty substance that helped with dehydration. Then, after seventy days, the body would be washed and rolled up in

linen, with fingers and toes being given special sheaths so that they didn't break. At some point, all this was deemed too much bother for someone who was, after all, dead. And we began to concentrate on pampering our bodies while we were still alive instead.

Expecting elderly kings to complete regular assault courses

There's a great, centuries-old European tradition of allowing elderly reigning monarchs to sit (or perhaps slump) on their throne right up until the bitter end. And if that means a five-year period during which they knocked feebly at death's door, then so be it. Ancient Egyptians, however, were more pragmatic; they thought that pharaohs ought to be able-bodied, and any physical decline should be kept firmly in check.

Hence the Heb-Sed, or the "Feast Of The Tail", which occurred during the pharaoh's thirtieth year in power and every three years subsequently. He would be expected to run up and down a specially laid out course, carrying various cumbersome objects; anyone who considers this cruel should bear in mind that it was previously common practice to simply murder them when they got too long in the tooth. Completion of the course would supposedly prove his physical fitness, although it's pretty certain that sycophantic priests would ensure that the pharaoh was awarded a pass mark even if he collapsed ten metres short of the finish line while clutching his chest. Thanks to democracy, we no longer need to put heads of state through such rigorous examinations – although it would be fun seeing some of them attempt the pole vault.

Punishing adulterers by inserting radishes into their anal passages

The phrase "revenge is a dish best served cold" hadn't yet been dreamt up by the poetic philosophers of Greco-Roman times. Curious legal quirks allowed certain victims to administer their own form of restorative justice to the person who had wronged them; Roman law supposedly gave you the right to rape a burglar who'd done over your property ("Er … right … couldn't we just put him in prison?") and in the case of adulterers in Greece, the cuckolded husband was permitted to retaliate as violently as his imagination would allow. Bearing in mind that colourful punishments of the ancient world included pouring molten metal down someone's throat, or cutting their nose off and putting them in a sack with a wild animal before dumping it in a river, you embarked on a relationship with another man's wife at your peril.

Some adulterers got away with their lives, but instead had to suffer the indignity of having a radish pushed up their anus. (Those who imagine that this could almost be a pleasurable experience have clearly never seen the size and shape of certain exotic types of radish.) How this punishment could have been meted out without it turning into an extended closing scene from the *Benny Hill Show* is unclear, and it's not something that we've chosen to carry forward to the modern era. At least, not outside the classified advertisements of some particularly tawdry magazines.

The hiring of professional mourners to wail at the graveside

On the one hand, paying for people to act particularly grief-stricken at a graveside is a despicable charade that insults the memory of the dear departed. On the other, the poor soul might not have had many friends, and few of those might bother turning up, let alone wail and cry at a decent volume. So why not give him a rousing send-off? Paid mourners became a part of funeral ceremonies in both Ancient Greece and Rome, and despite laws being passed to try to prevent the practice, it was probably quite hard to clamp down on. After all, if someone's a good enough actor to conjure up authentic-looking grief over someone they never knew, they're not going to find it difficult to put on an indignant face of denial if they're accused of being a professional mourner. It wasn't all ululation and flailing; rather like a master of ceremonies, they'd subtly coordinate the grief so that everyone would moan and shake their heads in sadness at the most suitable moments. Women were particularly skilled at it, and it's thought that the Greek attempts to abolish paid lamentation may have been partly to deprive women of the one opportunity they had to display some public power.

Paid mourning – which gave us the Latin word "placebo" – has re-emerged on a number of occasions since ancient times, but the money was poor, the work was depressing, and it never looked good on anyone's CV.

Exercising vigorously in public without wearing any clothes

If you take a moment to ponder which of the world's greatest sportsmen have achieved their biggest accolades while in the nude, you'll quickly realize that the answer is "none". Pelé didn't blast Brazil to World Cup glory while his shorts were still in the dressing room. Carl Lewis didn't set his indoor long jump record with dangling genitals impairing his aerodynamicism. They both wisely covered up.

The original Greek Olympics were, by contrast, notable for all the competitors being stark naked – save for the charioteers, who for some reason (perhaps they had a sick note) were allowed to keep their clothes on. The Greeks became very keen on exercising in the altogether around the sixth century BC, managing to convince athletes that it signified courage, strength and high status. Soon, it was de rigueur to be in the nude club, regardless of how minimally endowed you might have been. To be fair, the ensuing comparison of pecs and abs did give everyone the incentive to tone up, and it definitely saved on laundry bills. On the down side, bits tended to get in the way. This is where the Kynodesme came in: this thin leather strap would be tied around the excess foreskin at the end of the penis, and wrapped around the waist to expose the scrotum. Hm. Maybe better off naked, after all.

Showing an excessive reverence for the herb silphium

We'll never know how great silphium was: how it added untold pizzazz to chicken dishes, how efficacious it was against disease, how grazing herds couldn't get enough of it. Because in a seven hundred year period, the Greeks and Romans – both having been driven wild by its flavour – managed to harvest the herb to complete extinction. All we have left is its relative, asafoetida – but the Romans dismissed that as a pathetic pretender to its throne.

The Romans believed that they'd hit upon a panacea. Regardless of your ailments, a bit of silphium would sort you out – either the juice, the resin, or just pushing the plant itself up your back passage. But when you're fighting all your illnesses and seasoning all your food with the same plant, you're eventually going to come up against a mismatch of supply and demand. And for some reason, only a small strip of land (120 x 30 miles) in Northern Africa (now Libya) was able to sustain the plant. All attempts at taking seeds or cuttings and planting them elsewhere failed dismally. So the neighbouring city of Cyrene flourished enormously as a result of the nearby silphium crop, but suffered badly when it finally ran out. Legend has it that Nero secured the very last silphium plant, and he ate it. Thanks, Nero. Now we'll never know.

Cursing enemies by scratching a message on some lead and burying it

If you were up against someone else for a job, a fair maiden's hand or glorious triumph in a sporting event, keeping your fingers crossed and hoping for the best was never going to be enough. Your best bet was to visit your neighbourhood curse tablet maker, for a combination of engraving and black magic that would all but ensure your victory. Their size belied their supposedly enormous power; rectangular and between just six and ten centimetres long, they were made out of soft lead or pewter-like material and engraved with the curse you wished to place on someone. "Marcus Antonius", one might have read, "blind his eyes during our chariot race so he fails to notice a rapidly approaching obstacle, like a wall or something." You'd then pop around to Marcus Antonius's house under some fake pretext – perhaps borrowing a cup of silphium – and then, when he wasn't looking, wedge the tablet under the floor or between some bricks. He wouldn't stand a chance.

The more curses placed on the tablet, the more numerous the disasters that would befall its recipient – and extra damage could be caused by having the text written backwards. They were all ineffective, but perhaps the most tragic was the erotic curse tablet, which desperate men used to induce lust-crazed desire in women. It didn't work – and women continue to be unimpressed by small bits of lead or pewter to this day.

Engaging underage boys in sexual relationships

It makes sense to us to shield our young sons from the sexual advances of older men, and report such activity to the relevant authorities. Not so in Greek times; fathers would be sought out for permission to have a fling with their male offspring, and like the unenlightened fools that they were, they'd often grant it.

The seduction techniques employed were as moon-eyed as any modern teenager's; totally lacking in dignity, men would hang around the baths or the gym hoping to catch a glimpse of them, then in the evening they'd write reams of soppy poetry and sleep on their beloved's doorstep. With dad's permission, this would evolve into a relationship; not always sexual, but this was often encouraged, and particularly in Crete where they reckoned it was a brilliant idea to control the size of the burgeoning population. What was in it for the boys? Gifts, education, and when they passed into adulthood, a lifelong friendship, apparently. The Romans weren't averse to a spot of pederasty, either, but as time went on it was seen as an effeminate Greek way of doing things, and by AD390 it had been made illegal. It's unlikely that similar bans in place throughout the modern world will be lifted at any point in the near future.

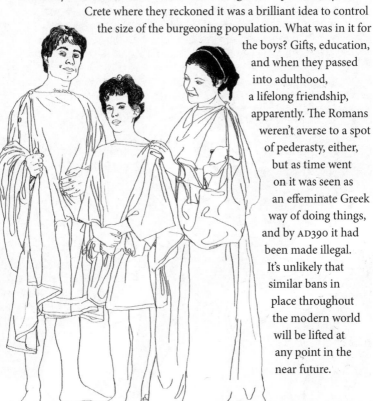

Trepanning: You need it like a hole in the head

"If it hurts, it's working." Well, if you're talking about vigorous exercise on a rowing machine, perhaps. But if you're referring to having a hole bored in your skull with a primitive drill well before the invention of effective anaesthetics, then probably not. Trepanation is the oldest known surgical procedure – there's evidence of it having been carried out back in the Neolithic Age, some eight thousand years BC – and also the most persistently, gloriously unsuccessful. You can't really blame self-proclaimed doctors from bygone ages for giving it a go if they had no access to ibuprofen capsules and were confronted with someone who had a headache; after all, if someone describes having pressure within their skull, it makes some kind of sense to let whatever's causing that pressure escape through a hole. But all that tended to escape was blood, bone and tissue. If the person somehow got better, they were going to get better despite the trepanning rather than because of it. If they didn't get better, additional holes would invariably be drilled or widened. At the height of trepanning's popularity amongst the medical profession, it's incredible that anyone bothered admitting to having a headache at all. And if they did make that error, they should surely have feigned a miraculous recovery when the drill was suddenly produced.

Hippocrates apparently returned from a trip to Marseille in the fourth century BC with news of the amazing head-drilling antics practised by the Gauls, and

went on to mention the procedure in his rib-tickling laughter compendium *On Wounds Of The Head*. But he didn't really shed much light on why and how it was deployed in Ancient Greece. By the Middle Ages, however, we know that it was used for all kinds of ailments – including, somewhat predictably, mental illness – and engravings of the time show unfortunate individuals with sunken eyes, tortured expressions and their heads clamped under a drill bit, looking for all the world as if they'd prefer to be attending a lovely birthday party instead.

You could say one thing only for trepanning, and that was the absolute consistency in the rate at which it despatched people to the grave: just a tad under a hundred percent. Some people lived to give other patients hope, certainly, but many more suffered hideous injury, brain damage or infection, and the ones who eagerly came back for repeat prescriptions – such as Prince Phillip of Orange at the turn of the seventeenth century – were few and far between.

Just when we appeared to have come to our senses in the twentieth century and finally abandoned the notion that pressure around the brain somehow needed to escape through holes, along came the concept of treating mental illness with frontal lobotomies, where the brain was once again probed with sharp instruments wielded by someone who didn't really know what they were doing. Occasionally, violent tendencies were calmed. More often, it would just create a different problem: zombie-like patients requiring constant care. The advent of antipsychotic drugs saw that particular medical fad abandoned, too, and has since been described as "one of the most barbaric mistakes ever perpetrated by mainstream medicine".

In the 1960s, trepanning was again mooted as a health benefit, mainly because of a Dutchman called Bart Huges who cited a supposedly successful trepanation that he had performed, somewhat bizarrely, upon himself. He believed that it increased "brain blood volume", which in turn precipitated a return to a childlike state of consciousness. To which you might well reply, well, I prefer my adultlike state of consciousness, to be honest. Of course, the vast majority of us – including the entire medical profession – are keen not to become the kind of person who gets evangelical about Neolithic surgical practices and so the rehabilitation of trepanning has been restricted to a few odd people lurking in remote corners of the Internet. "It's been around for ages," said one, in a lame attempt to justify it. Well, so has slavery, but you wouldn't necessarily recommend it to your mates.

Garnishing food with rotting fish entrails

Passing time travellers might well consider such supermarket fare as Marmite or Biltong as unpleasant, verging on inedible, but the Greek and Roman entry into the encyclopedia of inexplicable foodstuffs was garum. A mixture of fermented fish entrails and blood, they'd spread it liberally on all kinds of foodstuffs, both savoury and sweet, like fussy children who won't eat anything unless it's coated in a layer of tomato ketchup.

The Greeks invented it – although why and how anyone would have ever been tempted to take an initial bite of decaying fish guts is anyone's guess – but the Romans were the ones who fell in love with it; varieties ranged from liquamen (a high-class garum made from mackerel) to low-grade stuff called allec (whose contents must have been so rank as to traumatize the poor souls whose job it was to make it). Following complaints from local residents, the malodorous manufacturing process occurred well out of town – but that didn't dampen anyone's enthusiasm for eating the stuff. Because as we've learned from factory farming, the further away we are from the reality of the production process of food, the happier we are to shove it down our necks.

Attempting to give clothes that bluey-white freshness by using urine

The marauding Goths that Roman soldiers spent a significant amount of time battling against had worked out how to make soap. They mixed fat with potash to create a substance that could lift off stubborn dirt, be it from their bodies or their bloodied tunics. The Romans preferred to oil themselves up and scrape off grime with a piece of metal called a strigil, but when it came to cleaning clothes they made one critical alteration to the Gothic recipe. Instead of using fat, they used urine.

Urine is something that we try quite hard to keep well away from our clothes. We're taught from a very young age that wetting ourselves won't do our trousers any favours, and there's a reason for that: urine doesn't smell great. This didn't seem to deter the Romans, however, and convinced of its ability to restore freshness to linen, they'd collect urine in pots on the street from anyone who felt able to donate. One can only imagine the state of the clothes after they'd been soaked in piss, stamped on and wrung out – but the Romans never really stumbled across a better method, despite evidence that they knew about the existence of soap. Quite why they never tried fresh water, rather than wait for said water to pass through the human body, is something of a mystery.

Celebrating each year by swapping places with your employees

Most of us would love to try swapping places with our bosses for a bit, and dish out the kind of brutal criticism that they subject us to on a daily basis. So it's no wonder that the festival of Saturnalia was embraced so enthusiastically by Roman slaves, who were exempted from punishment for its duration, given the opportunity to show "disrespect" to their masters, and eat lordly feasts while being waited upon. Originally one day long, it ended up spanning six days of social chaos, where roles were reversed and general japery was perpetrated.

It would have been a miserable time for any slaves whose Scrooge-like masters chose not to observe Saturnalia for health and safety reasons, but there were aspects of the festival that everyone could enjoy; the giving of small gifts, the rare opportunity to gamble legally, and, according to Lucian, there was "singing naked, clapping of frenzied hands and occasional ducking of [faces] in icy water", which sounds like a good party by anyone's standards. Indeed, people had such a riotous time that Augustus attempted (unsuccessfully) to shorten it. Its position at the end of December saw it form the basis of modern Christmas celebrations once Christianity had taken hold in Europe. But don't ask to swap places with your boss this coming Yuletide, because he won't let you, the curmudgeonly sod.

Vomiting copiously at mealtimes without saying sorry

If you find yourself mopping up pools of vomit from under your dinner table this weekend, you'll probably reflect ruefully that your dinner party has not been the roaring success that you'd hoped. Not so at Roman banquets, where the size of the feasts required you to "make a bit more room"; as a result, any bowls of vomit lying around were a clear indication of the enormous success of the event rather than a sign that the chicken supreme hadn't been adequately heated through. As one source described Roman dining habits: "They vomit so they may eat, and they eat so they may vomit".

One can barely imagine the unpleasant scenes at such banquets, one person tucking into honeyed cakes while the next says "ooh, could do with a vomit" before retching violently. Not least because as primates we've evolved the wonderful act of sympathetic vomiting, where if our dining companions are doing it, we're likely to follow suit. Today it's considered polite to run rapidly from the room before heaving, and cycles of binging and vomiting are treated as a mental illness. Go figure.

Using elephants to fight your battles for you

If you were a soldier in Ancient Greece, the weary regularity of scrapping with your neighbours might have left you bored with the standard battlefield scenario – men, weapons, blood, the occasional tree. But when the Greeks confronted the Persians at the Battle of Gaugamela in 331 BC, they would have been utterly startled to see a deployment of elephants on the front line. It didn't work that well (the Greeks won) but Alexander the Great was mightily impressed by the psychological tactic, and adopted it for himself.

They're big. They look scary. They can carry loads of stuff. And by sitting on top of one, you get a great vantage point over the area. Over the next few hundred years, elephants were increasingly likely to find themselves lumbering onto the battlefield with slight concern etched on

their grey faces – and particularly the Sri Lankan variety, who were adjudged to be the most suitable for fighting alongside. But once the element of surprise had worn off, elephants started to become something of a liability. Someone discovered, for example, that they were rattled by the sound of squealing pigs, so by pouring oil on pigs, setting them on fire and unleashing them at the enemy, the elephants would begin stampeding and laying waste to their own side. Then, when gunpowder revolutionized the battlefield, elephants became such hilariously easy targets that they were finally allowed to retire gracefully to some leafy part of the Sri Lankan countryside.

Making major life decisions based on how birds fly past

The auspicium, or auspices, were the Roman equivalent of a cost-benefit analysis. Before any important decisions were taken, they would shun such laborious processes as weighing up pros and cons, and instead call on the services of the augur, whose readings of the patterns of birds in the sky would largely dictate the subsequent course of action. Wars were fought, unnecessary journeys embarked upon, inadvisable marriages entered into, all because of something as random and unpredictable as the direction in which deeply unintelligent birds chose to travel.

Of course, the augur would wield a huge amount of power as a result, and his pronouncements could be massively influenced by bribery, or indeed his own opinions. (Augurs would be fairly unlikely to predict their own executions, for example.) Those mistrustful of the augur might instead look to haruspex for guidance – an equally unreliable fortune-telling process, whereby the livers of sacrificed animals would be analyzed for bad omens. Unsurprisingly, no haruspex ever revealed that paying too much attention to the offal of a sheep might cause you to make incorrect life choices.

Disguising foods as other foods to create an element of surprise

Of all the emotions you'd want your dinner guests to experience, shock and disorientation come pretty low on the list. But the irritating Roman habit of disguising food as other food would turn a simple meal into a test of nerve, where items you expected to be eggs actually turned out to be cakes, and vice versa.

It's a trick we still play on kids for their own benefit – placing healthy ingredients into child-friendly arrangements, such as happy smiling faces or unthreatening burger shapes. But when Roman chefs disguised pork as chicken, or ham as doves, the only real reason for them to do so was to show off. They might take a date, remove the stone, then stick a cinnamon-covered almond back into it to make it look like a stone. A neat trick, until everyone refuses to eat the almond, because they think it's a stone, and you have to inform them that the stone is in fact an almond. About the only item that should have been reconstituted into a different form was the dormouse; Romans may have enjoyed snacking on them, but they'd have been an even bigger hit if they'd been molded into lozenge shapes and called Mouse Bars.

Picnicking gaily in graveyards

The festival of Parentalia – the honouring of the dead – took place in the gloomy month of February. Romans felt that this time of year portended all kinds of doom, and Parentalia gave everyone a chance to placate any spirits from beyond the grave who might have become irritated with them for some reason or other.

The final day of this festival was Feralia, on 21 February, where families would decamp to the graveyard and share a meal with their deceased relatives. Literally. A "libation pipe" led down to where the body was buried, and, despite the fact that the corpse was long past appreciating honey, milk or wine, they poured it down there regardless, in the hope of refreshing them for their subsequent year of death. No murmurs of "thank you kindly, I'll have another" came back up the

pipe, but the Romans assumed they were enjoying it, and continued the custom. Today, the only people who picnic in graveyards are goths – and not the marauding tribes of central Europe, just kids who listen to too much Marilyn Manson.

Showing muted interest in the welfare of one's own children

Contraceptives in Roman times were rubbish (see p.180) and abortion was pretty dangerous, so, instead, family planning measures were implemented after the child had actually been born. This doesn't seem to have been particularly controversial, either; fathers had the right to kill any inconvenient offspring if it interfered with their inheritance plans, or if they were going to be away fighting and unable to bring it up, or if it had been inconsiderate enough to be born a girl. Of course, murdering one's own child in cold blood isn't the most pleasant of activities, so they'd just leave the baby somewhere remote and wander off. Babies, tending not to be able to fend for themselves in the wild, or still less find they own way home, generally perished.

The other option was to grit your teeth for a few years, raise the child as best you could, and then sell it into slavery to make a bit of cash. While conceivably the more humane of the two options, life as a Roman slave wasn't much of a laugh – except perhaps during Saturnalia – and conquered foes of the Romans generally opted for suicide rather than a life of slavery. So kids were despatched to the galleys or the mines in exchange for a few silver coins. What loving father could do more?

Self-inflicted welts and chastity belts: The Dark and Middle Ages

The general consensus from those historians who know best is that the thousand years following the fall of the Roman Empire was a pretty unpleasant time to be alive. It's hard to draw meaningful comparisons with the present day – we may enjoy such luxuries as inflatable dinghies and ready-made pasta salads, but we still live under the threats of cancer and terrorism – but medieval times were grim by anyone's standards. Sure, there would have been glimmers of pleasure – the odd sunny day unblighted by disease, a lilting melody from a passing troubadour – but the years in question consisted largely of incessant toil, inadequate roofing and rough, shapeless clothing that not only failed to accentuate your hourglass figure, but also irritated the skin under your arms. Unless, of course, you were born into nobility, in which case life was all rare beef, silk and falconry.

So our list of idiosyncratic behaviours of medieval times can mainly be attributed to the appalling things people were having to cope with – grim illnesses, crop failure, and a particularly brutal feudal system which saw the gap between rich and poor stretch to unsustainable levels. You wouldn't have been very optimistic about things getting much better, either; the Renaissance was about to give everyone's prospects something of a boost, but no one knew if or when it was on its way. So waiting for it to arrive must have been gruelling, to say the least.

Flagellating yourself to atone for the sins of society

There still seems to be a belief that if you deliberately put yourself through a certain amount of physical discomfort, you'll emerge from the experience as a more well-rounded human being. True, many of us take the opposite approach by swaddling ourselves in a duvet and gorging on marshmallows – but we can still hear phrases in the back of our heads like "no pain no gain" or "if it hurts, it's working".

Groups of flagellants took this idea to something of an extreme back in the twelfth and thirteenth centuries; instead of just denying themselves the odd treat, they'd savagely and religiously beat themselves with whips in the hope that scarring themselves would eventually take some of the sting out of medieval life. The worse things got, the more flagellants would roam from town to town in militant pilgrimages; as famine took hold in Europe in the 1250s, Perugian flagellants began killing those who opposed their antics, for fear that they were in league with the devil, and the pope was forced to introduce a ban. But around a century later, with the Black Death in full swing, German flagellants returned to the practice with gusto – this time to musical accompaniment called *Geisslerlieder*. You could recreate this with a modern twist by walking down the high street and thrashing yourself with electric cable to the sound of "Beat It" by Michael Jackson, but it's unlikely you'll get many of your fellow citizens joining in.

Tucking into a tasty dinner of swan in chaudon sauce

There's a vague correlation between the attractiveness of an animal and the likelihood of us roasting it on an open fire. We tuck happily into cows and pigs, while giraffes and peacocks are notable by their absence from popular cookery books. (Quite why animals haven't all evolved extraordinary plumage in order to stay out of the butcher's and off our dinner tables is worth pondering, extremely briefly.) So the swan, because of its graceful neck and snow-white feathers, has thus managed to avoid being widely eaten since medieval times, when aristocrats would happily chow down on mouth-watering recipes such as this:

For to dihyte a swan. Tak & vndo hym & wasch hym, & do on a spite & enarme hym fayre & roste hym wel; & dysmembre hym on þe beste manere & mak a fayre chyne, & þe sauce þerto schal be mad in þis manere, & it is clept: Chaudon.

A myth still circulates that the Queen owns all the swans in Britain and that it's an act of treason to eat them. In fact, they're just protected under the UK's Wildlife and Countryside Act – as are many other species. But back in 1391, the appointment of a "Keeper of the King's Swans" made people think twice about having swan fricassee, just in case they were to incur the wrath of Richard II. They tended to just have some chicken instead.

Living every day as if it's your last

This is a phrase that we use to describe unabashed extroverts who bungee jump off tall buildings, spend money like water and make inexplicably successful advances to members of the opposite sex who are, theoretically, way out of their league. We partly admire them for their gall, while also mocking their stupidity and being glad that we have some savings, some dignity and all our limbs intact. But citizens of medieval Europe lived every day as if it was their last because, well, it might just have been.

You wouldn't have been eager to get into the life insurance business back then. All the awful endings that could befall the average human – war, starvation, plague, being accused of a minor crime (see p.170) – reduced life expectancy to depressingly low levels, and proud great-grandparents were pretty thin on the ground. The Danse Macabre, a medieval allegory featuring skeletal representation of everyone from barons to bakers, was a subtle reminder to people from all walks of life to be prepared for death, and texts such as the *Ars Moriendi* (or Art of Dying) advised people that hey, actually, dying isn't so bad – for one thing, it's a blessed relief from worrying about anything bubonic – and went on to give a few hints on how to "die well" (that is, don't make too much of a fuss, because dying is a perfectly normal thing to do, after all).

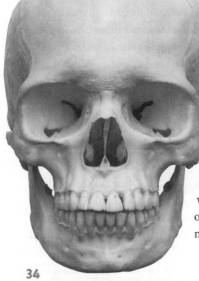

Covering up foul odours in the hope it would ward off disease

While we have a compulsion to recoil from powerful smells – sewage, rotting fish, Giorgio Beverly Hills perfume (see p.100) – getting a whiff of these odours doesn't actually do us any harm (unless of course we're talking carbon monoxide or mustard gas). But the belief that noxious airs, or miasmas, were responsible for the outbreak of disease was prevalent from ancient times, even until the time of Florence Nightingale. Occasionally, some dangerous crank from the Far East would suggest that perhaps germs had something to do with it, but we'd smugly bat their suggestions away and focus our attention on getting rid of smells.

Of course, odours are removed by cleaning, which in itself is helpful in preventing disease. This may be why the miasma theory persisted for so long: it was almost right, but not quite. But this crucial error allowed diseases like cholera to run rampant for much longer than they should have done. What with people dropping dead of bubonic plague throughout the fourteenth century, the "pocket full of posies" (as immortalized in the children's rhyme) formed an ineffective front line of defence against the plague; today we deploy antibiotics instead, and for all their drawbacks, they're substantially more successful than a nosegay or pomander.

Establishing someone's innocence by torturing them

Don't think "innocent until proven guilty" – think "subjected to unbearable pain until such time as your innocence has been determined by a process as random as flipping a coin". With such a terrifying lose-lose legal system as "trial by ordeal" in operation, your fear wasn't of being found guilty – it was of being unfortunate enough to be accused in the first place. Noblemen who might or might not have committed a crime would have been made to hold a red-hot iron bar, or walk across hot coals; if their badly burned extremities didn't show signs within three days that God was helping them heal, they'd be pronounced

guilty. As antiseptic wasn't that plentiful in medieval times, conviction rates tended to be high. Common folk, meanwhile, would be invited to plunge their hand into a cauldron of boiling water, or oil, to retrieve a stone, to which their reply must surely have been "Oh no, must I?" A neat take on ordeal by water was to throw someone in a river with a heavy weight attached, with survivors proclaimed innocent – although witches suffered from a neat switcheroo to this plan (see p.69).

Trial by combat was another quaint but highly dangerous legal process, where the innocent of two parties was deemed the one who managed to beat the other one in a fight. If you were fit, healthy and good at scrapping, you'd get away with murder – although, strangely, women, elderly and the infirm could nominate someone to fight on their behalf. Trial by combat was still legal in Britain until 1819, but the jury system became standard in the twelfth century – much to the relief of weedy criminals across the land.

Composing riddles

If someone came up to you at a house party and introduced themselves by saying "My first is in castle, my second in moat, my third is in river, but never in boat" – you might reasonably ask him to shut up before mooching off into the kitchen. There's a sneering edge of superiority about a riddle – "I know what I'm going on about, you work it out" – and it's no coincidence that there are Norse tales of gods vanquishing foes by posing particularly baffling riddles. Striking them down with thunderbolts would probably be faster, but Odin in particular seemed keener on mental humiliation.

Medieval riddles, or enigmata, while still requiring a bit of brainpower to solve, weren't quite as irritating, as their purpose was more bawdy double entendre than bamboozlement. In their seventh- and eighth-century heyday, hinting at sexual topics in verse wasn't really the done thing, but if you could pretend it had a weighty subtext you'd probably get away with it; the phrase "fair maiden filled me with breath" might have had people fainting with shock, until you pointed out that you were actually talking about a wind instrument. Aah. I see. The collection of one hundred or so of these riddles in the *Exeter Book* – the most notable collection of Old English writing – has turned them into something of a distinguished literary form, but these days we vastly prefer our puzzles to come in jigsaw format.

Getting a barber to pull out your troublesome tooth

You'd be unlikely to let your butcher do your accounts, or your bank manager to give you a pedicure, and of all the people you might choose to extract a rotting tooth or remove your appendix, your hairdresser would have to come pretty low on the list. But in medieval times that's just how it was; in theory, monks had the job of performing operations on fellow humans but an inconvenient papal decree actually forbade them from spilling blood, which rather reined in their surgical ambitions. So they had to find assistance from people who had a handy set of sharp cutting implements; barbers got the job whether they had the skills to deploy these tools or not, and they set about sticking sharp objects into us with gusto.

People are nervous enough about going for a dental appointment these days, despite the availability of both local and general anaesthetics on hand to stop us screaming, and a dentist with a few letters after their name. But back then, the choice was stark: either continue putting up with the pain you're suffering, or see someone who has a slim chance of being able to sort it out. By 1308 the Worshipful Company of Barbers had been founded in England, cutting both our hair and our skin as necessary, and in 1540 the Company of Barber Surgeons acknowledged their status. Barbers still retain the red and white striped pole outside their premises, as a reminder of the time when they'd do much worse than accidentally nick your ear with some clippers.

Locking your wife's genitalia up for safe keeping

With rape a regular occurrence in the middle ages, travelling soldiers managed to persuade their female partners that the cast-iron chastity belt was an important personal protection device that should be worn for their own safety. Of course, it had the convenient side effect of severely limiting the woman's sexual freedom, which would have been a boon for men of a severely jealous disposition. Of course, a soldier had carte blanche to rape and pillage as he liked while gallivanting abroad, but back at home his wife would be struggling with clumsy, slightly rusting metal underwear that allowed stuff to get out but, crucially, allowed nothing to get in.

A visiting Italian noted that British men of this period were either "the most discreet lovers in the world, or incapable of love," while women were "very violent in their passions" – so maybe men believed they had cause to be concerned about the rampant sexuality of their wives. But locking up a woman's genitals isn't the soundest base for a loving relationship, and while chastity belts were still knocking about until late in the nineteenth century, this was more to keep a check on masturbatory habits (see p.72) than to prevent extramarital liaisons.

Predicting the future using sand

Every era has its hare-brained methods of attempting to predict the future, all of them singularly unsuccessful and always superseded by something equally lacking in scientific reasoning. The auspices of Roman times (see p.27) were replaced with geomancy, a method of divining that had made its way from Islamic countries of the Middle East during the eleventh century. What geomancy had going for it was its sheer complexity; its interpretation of patterns of sand or soil depended on referring to various indices, matrices and tables, which considerably boosted its credibility.

Geomancy was said to deal with straightforward yes-or-no questions best of all (presumably because it had a fifty-fifty chance of success)

Jokes that aren't as funny as they were at the time

There wasn't a great deal to laugh about in the Middle Ages. People occasionally fell over on their arses, sure. Children did pathetic but endearing impressions of Ethelred the Unready. Dogs sneezed. People made amusing quips that made the passing months seem a little less tortuous – but the few examples of said humour that have filtered down to the present day certainly couldn't be worked into a sitcom script or a stand-up routine, lest the audience start to turn nasty and loudly voice their disapproval. Here's an example from the oldest surviving joke book called the *Philogelos*, written by a thigh-slapping double act called Hieorcles and Philagrus in around the fourth century AD.

> *An intellectual was eating dinner with his father. On the table was a large lettuce with many succulent shoots. The intellectual suggested: "Father, you eat the children; I'll take mother."*

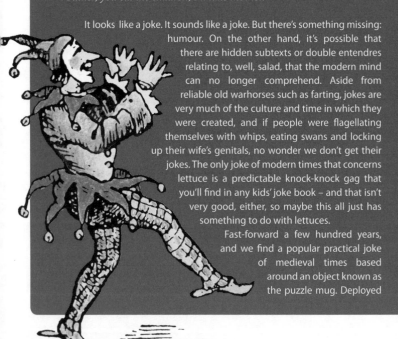

It looks like a joke. It sounds like a joke. But there's something missing: humour. On the other hand, it's possible that there are hidden subtexts or double entendres relating to, well, salad, that the modern mind can no longer comprehend. Aside from reliable old warhorses such as farting, jokes are very much of the culture and time in which they were created, and if people were flagellating themselves with whips, eating swans and locking up their wife's genitals, no wonder we don't get their jokes. The only joke of modern times that concerns lettuce is a predictable knock-knock gag that you'll find in any kids' joke book – and that isn't very good, either, so maybe this all just has something to do with lettuces.

Fast-forward a few hundred years, and we find a popular practical joke of medieval times based around an object known as the puzzle mug. Deployed in taverns on unsuspecting regulars who had already drunk too much, the gag involved a ceramic vessel with discreetly placed holes bored in it; when someone tried to take a swig without covering the correct holes with their fingers, they'd get covered in beer. Cue widespread hilarity. It probably won't ever stop being funny to see someone accidentally fail to get some drink into their mouths, but it's not quite as funny if you know that it's coming. Today, we'd be more likely to warn them of the puzzle mug's idiosyncrasies in order to avoid scenes of social embarrassment.

Shakespeare's jokes used many of the devices we still use to make each other laugh – allusions to sexual activity, withering criticism, excruciating puns – but we tend not to understand his jokes unless they're flagged up in bold type in a book of English-Language exam revision notes, or signposted with exuberant smiles and expansive gestures by a couple of enthusiastic actors. The Georgian era saw a collection of one-liners in the 1739 book *Joe Miller's Jests* which, again, had recognizable themes running through it (the supposed stupidity of the Irish, people lying about their age, titillating mentions of women from certain parts of the country who have loose sexual morals) but the very fact that these 250 jokes were published in book format meant that they very quickly lost their cachet; any rubbish old joke eventually came to be known as a "Joe Miller" as a result. But the Victorians, for all their alleged humourlessness, did have the odd joke that was verging on comprehensible, even funny, to the modern ear.

> *"Look here, Mary, this steak is quite black. How do you account for it?"*
> *"Well, sir, I don't rightly know, sir, unless it's because the cook's uncle just died."*

Bm-tsh! By the 1930s, we start getting shaggy dog stories that form the basis of the rambling comic monologues we hear today, then post-war we see an explosion of elephant gags, injured baby gags, filthy jokes, bumper stickers, and forwarded emails which come in the form "You know you're ____ when you've ____." Of course, jokes are never as funny as when we heard them the first time. And it's something of a tribute to the human mind that we're still able to make each other laugh after several millennia of sitting around feeling a bit bored and trying to be funny.

rather than imponderables such as "why don't nice girls like me?" which were far harder to assess via sand analysis. It took until the 1600s for humans to completely lose faith in the pronouncements of the geomancer, and while we might be surprised that the practice lasted even that long, you only have to look at the substantial earnings of tabloid astrologers to know that we're still desperate to believe that our lives are guided by an otherworldly force, and at the time the geomancer gave as good a reassurance as any. Today, you can recreate the uncertainty of medieval times by purchasing geomancy software, which reduces all the complex number crunching into one handy mouse click.

Going out for the evening to catch a morality play

If we describe anyone other than a man of the cloth as "preaching" to us, it's not generally meant in a positive way. Most of us develop an aversion to being told what to do or how to behave as we grow up, and if we felt that a form of entertainment was explicitly suggesting that we ought to buck up and improve our moral outlook, we'd probably feel a bit insulted.

It's possible that audiences had grown tired of being force-fed biblical stories via the mystery plays of the earlier Middle Ages, but theatre companies continued to work Christian values into the new breed of morality plays – didactic works that featured characters representing humanity and other characters representing virtues or vices, that panned out to recommend the virtues and expose the vices as inadvisable. The audience would, presumably, walk away with a renewed commitment to not covet their neighbour's wife – at least for a couple of days – and thus the morals of the nation were, somewhat loosely, upheld. Modern films still tend to depict the triumph of good over evil, but it's not so much to keep a check on our behaviour as to make us feel slightly less depressed about the state of the world.

Restoring one's virginity by bathing in water infused with comfrey

The sanctity of female virginity was greatly respected in medieval times, and losing it as a consequence of succumbing briefly to forces of lust was deeply frowned upon. Of course, victims of rape were looked upon with a certain amount of sympathy; and the French scholar Jean Gerson even had words of solace for women who lost their moral fortitude in a moment of passion, claiming that if they repented and confessed their sin, that virginity would somehow be restored.

But of course, there's a physical sign of a woman no longer being a virgin, and restoring that was always going to be rather trickier. In such circumstances, women would turn to comfrey, the wonder herb of the era. Plentiful on British riverbanks, it was exalted for its healing properties, and was sometimes known as "knitbone" for its supposed ability to mend fractures. But it was also supposed to have the power to replace a broken hymen. Women would sit in a bath of water infused with comfrey – a giant cup of tea, effectively – in the hope that the hymen would grow back. It didn't, but they kept doing it anyway. Today, comfrey is still valued, but more for its fertilizing properties. Plants, that is.

Persecuting sufferers of acne, as if they're not suffering enough already

If half the people in your neighbourhood suddenly dropped dead of a mysterious disease, you'd want to know what was causing it, and how best you could protect yourself against your armpits swelling up, and unexpectedly vomiting blood. But as we've seen already in this chapter, flagellating oneself or masking foul odours didn't do very much to help against the Black Death, and society was at a loss as to where to pin the blame. While it was generally accepted that the wrath of God had something to do with it, blaming God wasn't really an option – not least because no one knew precisely where God lived. So other innocent parties got it in the neck instead.

It's perhaps predictable that Jewish communities were among the first to suffer; they were accused of poisoning the water supply, and were slaughtered en masse in Strasbourg, Mainz and Cologne. "Friars, foreigners, beggars and pilgrims" also found themselves unreasonably picked on. But those with mild skin afflictions would have felt most mistreated. In the rush to stamp out the plague, lepers were slaughtered, followed by anyone who looked a bit leper-y, including sufferers of psoriasis, acne, and congested complexion, which, of course, isn't remotely contagious. In a final blow to the quarter of European citizens who perished at the hands of the Black Death, cats were killed for being in league with the devil – when they might have been the one species that could have helped by killing the rats that were spreading the disease.

Practising archery without due care and attention

The arrival of advanced longbow tactics on the battlefield in the early fourteenth century came as something of a shock to soldiers who thought that they were at a safe distance from the enemy, but suddenly found themselves annoyingly slaughtered by a blizzard of arrows. At the Battle of Crécy in 1346, some two thousand French knights were killed by English archers for the loss of a mere fifty men – thus proving the total dominance in combat of sharp things flying through the air extremely rapidly.

Of course, weapons develop and improve over time, and there's nothing unusual or odd about the coming and going of the bow and arrow. But what was slightly odd *was* how its importance changed people's weekends. The "Assize of Arms" already made it compulsory for all Englishmen between the ages of fifteen and sixty to equip themselves with bows and arrows, but Edward III went further in 1363 by ordering the practice of archery on Sundays and public holidays, which must have been a total drag for anyone with a hangover. As if to underline the importance of improving the skills of rookie archers, it was also the case that if you accidentally killed someone while practicing, it didn't really count as a punishable offence. It was probably a good idea not to accidentally annoy anyone at archery practice.

Paying someone to compensate for the injury you inflicted on them

For those who thought the biblical approach to redress – an eye for an eye, a tooth for a tooth – was unnecessarily brutal, the medieval concept of weregild offered a more practical and peaceful alternative; namely eight shillings for a tooth, and 66 shillings, 6 pence and a third of a penny for an eye. In a neat precursor of today's compensation culture, the ninth century laws of Alfred the Great laid out various remunerations to be paid to the victims or families of victims – including, for example, six shillings to be handed over if your dog got out of control and bit someone. No lengthy legal procedures, no weighing up the potential loss of earnings, no putting a value on wounded pride or the cost of a recuperative holiday in Wessex – just a flat fee.

Things became slightly more complex in the case of murder; you couldn't just buy forgiveness for having disembowelled someone in a wooded glade, but you would have to pay compensation to the family as well as receive your punishment. If you were stupid enough to kill a prince, you'd be talking 1500 shillings. Farmers came in a bit cheaper at a mere 100, while the 40–88 shillings paid to the families of serfs probably came in pretty useful; having a few expendable, mouthy serfs in your family who were likely to annoy fearsome men with big fists was probably a pretty good insurance policy.

Rising up against the ruling classes

There's a difference between protesting and revolting. The former ranges from penning a mildly disgruntled letter to your local newspaper, to participating in a march chaperoned by a few hundred police officers while you wave a banner and shout about what you want, and when you want it. A revolt, however, abandons any social niceties, swells with thousands upon thousands of furious people, and gets pretty bloody scary.

In a sense, those who participated in the dozens of peasants' rebellions throughout Europe in the fouteenth century didn't really have much choice, and certainly had nothing to lose; when lives are so ravaged by disease, poverty and rampant envy of the undeserving upper classes, anger is pretty much all you've got left. Tragically, and despite their size and ferocity, every one of those revolts – including the best-documented one in Britain in 1381 – ended in failure, and the word "peasant" gained all its pejorative meanings. The noblemen with the power, money and prestige always came out on top, the ringleaders of the revolt were soundly punished, and all those who had got excited about the prospect of a more equal and prosperous society were dispatched back whence they came, to experience greater inequality and considerably less prosperity. Democracy may have initially felt quite powerful, but eventually we became cynical about that too, and started writing impotent letters to the local newspaper instead.

Being a soldier while also showing respect towards women

Anyone who chooses to fight for their country has always had reserves of courage and loyalty that put cowards like the rest of us – who, after all, depend on their bravery – to shame. But when you assemble several thousand men in a combat situation, the ensuing flood of testosterone has traditionally resulted in a less-than-respectful attitude towards women. The concept of rape as one of the spoils of war was a constant for many centuries; today, you get the unedifying spectacle of glamour models being flown out to remote war zones to give sex-starved squaddies something to briefly drool over.

Medieval knights, however, combined that courage and loyalty with a gallantry that required them "to do nothing to displease maidens". It's not clear why a bloke with a sword on a horse should have more respect for women than a bloke not on a horse, but their duties were to protect the weaker and more vulnerable members of society, and to serve ladies, rather than smack them on the rear as they were passing. Their code of honour also required them to

refrain from "baseness", which presumably precluded them from shouting "Phwoooaargh!" at women they fancied. The sheer effort of maintaining this attitude towards the fairer sex eventually proved too much, and while raping and pillaging are no longer officially sanctioned, you'd have to say that chivalry is now a bit thin on the ground, too.

Informing people that there are animals who can lay waste to forests with burning dung

"Here begins the book of the nature of beasts," begins a medieval book about the nature of beasts, "of lions, and panthers, and tigers, wolves and foxes, dogs and apes." And snakes with wings, and hedgehogs with grapes on their backs, and horned animals that casually throw themselves off mountains. The thing about compiling a book about animals in medieval times is that the writers didn't have the resources available to the likes of

David Attenborough. Rather like Chinese whispers, information about various exotic animals and what they looked like was passed from person to person, with descriptions becoming ever more distorted, so that by the time they were immortalized on the page crocodiles ended up looking more like dogs, and ostriches appeared to have hooves.

You can't blame the creators of these "bestiaries" for lack of accuracy, but some of the more outlandish claims must have rung alarm bells in even the most credulous and unsceptical of minds. The manticore – a fearsome combination of lion, scorpion and man – took its place in the bestiary alongside doves and pelicans. And the bonnacon, a bison-like creature, was said to emit toxic flatulence and faeces that scorched the landscape. It's a feat to which many men would lay claim today, but it wasn't until more enlightened times that the fearsome effluence of the bonnacon was revealed to be the figment of a rather over-active imagination.

Baking an extra loaf of bread for fear of being imprisoned, or worse

With today's miracles of technology, it's possible to shove the ingredients for making bread into a machine, and have a just-about-adequate loaf emerge some two hours later. But we still value the craft of the baker; they're simply better at it than we are, and in times where decent ovens – and, indeed, electric baking devices with paddle attachments – were scarce, the baker held something of a monopoly over the whole bread production process. And as a result the odd evil baker would exploit his position by making disappointingly small loaves, or padding them out with sand.

The Assize of Bread and Ale, introduced in England in the mid-thirteenth century, finally gave some protection to the consumer by stipulating exactly how much bread you got for your buck. A sliding scale of fines was imposed on the baker, depending on by how much he'd defrauded his customers, and persistent offenders would be punished by being stuck in the local pillories to be pelted with any convenient objects that were lying nearby. The ultimate punishment was the Baker's Baptism; being submerged in a nearby river for as long as the presiding official thought it necessary. (Also known as "drowning".) Bakers hurriedly overcompensated to avoid punishment, hence the baker's dozen; you were given thirteen for the price of twelve. Just in case.

Placing a curse on a book in order to dissuade thieves from nicking it

Copying a book these days can be as simple as an alt-click-drag on a computer desktop. Before the printing press, the process took several million times longer, and a copy of a book was, inevitably, vastly more precious as a result. Theft of manuscripts by bibliomaniacs with a hunger for knowledge or, more likely, an urge to sell the book on for a few hundred shillings, was a constant threat, and a security system had to be devised that would dissuade people from such thievery. Simply blessing the book or praying for its safety had little effect, but the introduction of a deterrent in the form of a written curse was a great deal more successful.

It was the one part of the book where the scribe had free rein to use his own imagination and write whatever he wanted, and the variety of punishments dreamt up for thievery were magnificently vicious. "Let him be struck with palsy", wrote one, "and all his members blasted". Nasty. "Let bookworms gnaw his entrails", read another. Rather than risk the possibility of having one's entrails gnawed by bookworms, thieves tended to steer clear and concentrate on a target that hadn't been inscribed with phrases like "let him be frizzled in a pan". Like pans, for example.

Bleeding to death and malodorous breath: 1450–1650

The arrival of the Renaissance coupled a welcome diminishing of the likelihood of succumbing horribly to the Black Death with huge advances in intellectual rigour. But a revolution in thought doesn't happen overnight; scientists may well have made huge strides forward in their understanding of the workings of the human body, but they continued to recommend the application of leeches to get rid of "bad blood". And as "being a bit scientific" became trendy, gentleman hobbyists took up the cause with gusto, spending far too much time attempting to turn everyday substances into gold – probably more motivated by the possibility of having something named after them than the advancement of humanity.

Developments in the arts brought a new realism in painting, and the emergence of complex polyphony in music would one day give birth to respected works by such renowned artistes as the Spice Girls (see p.187). While people waited fruitlessly for such sonorous delights to evolve, however, they had to pluck ineptly at hurdy-gurdies. But on the whole, life was looking up – unless you were a woman with a passion for acting, in which case theatrical etiquette dictated that you had to sit grumpily through plays, watching vastly inferior male thespians battling their way across the stage in gaudy dresses and unconvincing high voices.

Punishing one's wife with disproportionate acts of violence

It would be safe to say that wife-beating isn't as socially acceptable as it used to be. Lawful disagreements with one's spouse consist of a blazing row plus finger wagging, and, thankfully, the authorities refuse to sanction any kind of domestic violence. Some generations of women, however, lived in fear of being slapped about by their husbands if they transgressed unwritten rules – and not necessarily because the men were psychopathic thugs, but because that's just how things were. Common law in Britain once permitted men to inflict "moderate correction" upon their wives (with the dubious reasoning that men have to "answer for their misbehaviour") thus bracketing them with unruly children and servants who dare to answer back; for example, "nagging" women might be paraded around town in a brank – an iron mask that clamped onto the head with a metal bar going into the mouth, while women who "conned" a man into marriage by using excessive make-up (see p.48) or "lift-and-separate" undergarments to lure him into the relationship, could equally expect to be on the receiving end of some kind of vicious discipline.

Sir William Blackstone's *Commentaries of The Laws of England* (1765) marks the decline of the law:

> *"In the politer reign of Charles II, this power of correction began to be doubted … Yet the lower rank of people, who were always fond of the old common law, still claim and exert their ancient privilege, and the courts of law will still permit a husband to restrain a wife of her liberty."*

The methods of restraint that were permitted are unclear, but seem to have been anything up to the point at which the woman started bleeding. But courts were even lenient on men who had "unintentionally" beaten their wives to death. An undeniably effective, some might say ultimate restraint, but now frowned upon by the European Convention on Human Rights.

Turning a mythological animal into a dining sensation

The cockatrice was an animal that appeared in medieval bestiaries (see p.60), but it's not clear whether Renaissance thinking had yet managed to convince people that this mythical half-lizard, half-rooster was merely a figment of someone's over-active imagination, or whether gaggles of them were thought to lurk in nearby forests at the dead of night. Had the cockatrice existed, you'd have had good reason to be scared of it; it had a deadly gaze that could either turn you to stone or kill you – depending on how vicious it was feeling – and touching it or even being breathed upon by it led to a similar fate. Only the humble weasel, it seems, was immune to its attacks – a clear indication that the authors of the bestiaries were making it up as they went along.

Anyway, whether it was to display supremacy over the non-existent cockatrice or simply because it was funny, Tudor cooks decided that reconstructing one out of available materials (er, dead farm animals) and serving it up for dinner would be a magnificent idea. Pig and chicken were spliced together in a vague approximation of rooster'n'lizard, and the resulting winged pork delicacy would be cooed over by wealthy diners. Today, the cockatrice has been banished to the realms of video games such as *Fighting Fantasy* (as a much-feared adversary, rather than an enormous dinner).

Making sure you didn't have too much blood going around your body

"Better out than in" goes the well-known saying, normally uttered when a friend is lurching violently from side to side after too much gin, and looks dangerously like performing the traditional multicoloured yawn. There may well be some medical sense in emptying the contents of your stomach under such circumstances, but bloodletting – which worked on a similar principle of ridding the body of its excesses, except with blood rather than vomit – certainly didn't do any good. Despite that, for hundreds of years medical experts drained off gallon after gallon of blood in the hope of curing various ailments. The more blood the better. If the patient fainted, they figured it was working, but if the draining was over-enthusiastic, the patient would die. Whoops.

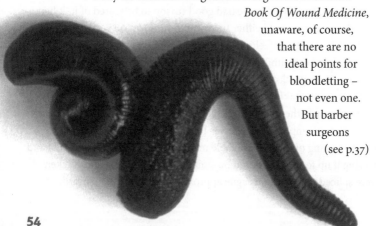

In 1517 surgeon Hans von Gersdorff listed the ideal points of the body for administering bloodletting in his book *Field Book Of Wound Medicine*, unaware, of course, that there are no ideal points for bloodletting – not even one. But barber surgeons (see p.37)

enthusiastically embraced the practice, and set about vigorously wounding unhealthy people in a bloodthirsty manner. In 1628, William Harvey stumbled upon the secret of circulation and the function of the heart, effectively disproving the bloodletting theory – but it took at least two hundred more years for doctors to admit that siphoning off someone's blood resulted in nothing more than a big bucket full of someone's blood.

Letting your teeth rot away as an indicator of social standing

It's hard for us, what with our clearly demarcated tradition of savoury main course followed by a sweet, to understand what it must have been like six hundred years ago when all dishes had an unbearably cloying sugariness running through them. Today, jars of fruity mincemeat go into mince pies at Christmas, but back then mincemeat did actually contain meat – something as alien to the modern palate as haddock in lemonade. Honey was once the universal sweetener, but when the Spanish started cultivating sugar cane in the West Indies and shipping it over to Britain, those who could afford it went mad for it. Potatoes

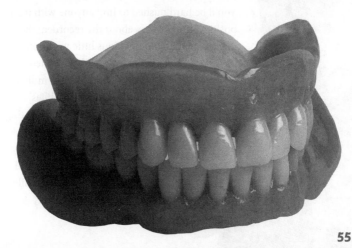

and tomatoes, sure – but sugar, that's what we really wanted to get our teeth into.

From then on it became a race to ingest as much sugar as possible, with the evidence of one's sweet tooth simply being how black said tooth had become; those whose budgets couldn't stretch to sucking raw sugar cane hastily turned to cosmetics to get their teeth blackened and thus elevate their social status. Strangely, while people knew that the blackened state of their teeth was directly related to all the sugar they'd ingested, no one seemed to care about the associated decay and hideously painful abscesses. Ironically, the poor (who were left to subsist on vegetables) had comparatively pearly white gnashers – an incredibly rare example of the socially deprived classes accidentally obtaining a minor health advantage.

Learning to play the recorder without being forced to by a teacher

Outside certain music colleges with whole departments dedicated to the authentic recreation of the music of the Renaissance, you'll be hard pushed to find anyone with many positive things to say about the recorder. These plastic tubes with precious little variation in dynamics or volume have ended up being manufactured in their millions, resulting in school assemblies resonating to a shrill, unrelenting noise wrapping itself around popular hymn tunes. Twenty-first-century parents are still putting up with this racket while wearing an unholy grimace, because they imagine it's affording their offspring the chance of a career as an internationally acclaimed instrumentalist, destination Sydney Opera House.

But before the plastic tube with holes, there was a wooden tube with holes. And by all accounts it didn't sound much better back then, either. To be fair to the recorder-makers of the time, no wind instruments were at a very advanced stage of development, and to the modern ear an ensemble of crumhorns, sackbuts, trumpets and recorders would have sounded like a disease-stricken farmyard. With the advent of the flute and clarinet in the 1700s, composers gratefully abandoned the recorder, where it languished in obscurity until it was embraced by enthusiastic modern-day music teachers, the fiends.

Encasing the male genitalia in a codpiece

"What should I do with my genitals?" isn't a question that modern men really have to ask, unless they're posing for a nude life drawing class. But the evolution of below-the-waist fashion in the sixteenth century posed a tricky problem for gentlemen, as, while their legs were adequately covered by hose, their genitals required their own separate garment to avoid them waggling about in the open air. What was initially just a "small bag with a flap" evolved into an extraordinary celebration of the male member, with any individual's inadequacies concealed behind constructions of awesome proportions.

Outside the rock star fraternity, few modern men feel the need to make their genitals bulge fearsomely in their trousers, for fear of alienating their fellow office workers or just being arrested for gross indecency. No such problem during the reign of Henry VIII, who positively encouraged men to have their codpieces "puffed and slashed", and even "ornamented with jewelled pins," for goodness sake. In extreme cases, the protuberance at the front of the codpiece was decorated with a face as if it was some kind of massive, inquisitive

tortoise, which presumably impressed women of the day, although it's hard to know why. When Elizabeth I came to the throne, she attempted to rein in some of this rampant masculinity by frowning upon the codpiece, and her disapproval led to it virtually disappearing by the turn of the seventeenth century, to be replaced by garments that thankfully signposted the penis a little less flamboyantly.

Wearing ruffs so big that especially long spoons had to be produced

Ruffs take their rightful place in a long line of impractical fashions, including the toga, the kynodesme (see p.18), the stiletto heel and the miniskirt (see p.126). When they came into fashion in the sixteenth century, it was almost inevitable that people would succumb to the mistaken belief that bigger is better, and before long the ruff around the Elizabethan neck had expanded to as much as eighteen inches in diameter, making the wearer look – in the words of a popular British sitcom – as if they'd "swallowed a plate". A Puritan writer by the name of Philip Stubbes made his feelings plain about the fashion in 1583, noting firstly that they'd been "invented by the devil" (distinctly possible) before going on to describe how they would "flip flap in the winde".

No matter how much starch had been applied to these gigantic ruffs to make them stand proud, a light shower could also quickly convert them into an inadequate shoulder concealer. To combat this, a wire frame was invented to offer support to the ruff in all weathers, when a more sensible solution might have been to abandon it altogether. The Dutch valiantly continued the fashion well into the seventeenth century, by which time everyone else had switched to the wing collar, which offered the twin benefits of not requiring heavy starching, and not making you look like an idiot.

Propping up the ailing British cap industry

These days, we almost exclusively rely on foreign nations to clothe us. If we burned everything in our wardrobe that was manufactured outside the country we live in, we'd probably be walking around town wearing only a scarf knitted by our mum and a pair of gloves knitted by our aunt. Which wouldn't only be a bit chilly, but probably illegal, too. The importing of clothing in Elizabethan times, however, had become a menace to society. Concerned by the quantity of cash that was leaving the country to purchase foreign silks and other "vain devices", and indeed the huge debts run up by vainglorious citizens who were desperate to get their hands on the latest fashions, Elizabeth I

Make-up whose use is no longer sanctioned by the British Skin Foundation

Tarting ourselves up to look nice is something we've done ever since the existence of rival lovers; however much we adore our partner, we're depressingly likely to have our attention distracted by someone who is smiling in our direction and who has gone to the trouble of making their eyelashes look longer, or their complexion healthier, or their underarms smoother or more fragrant. The idea of what constitutes beauty has obviously varied over the centuries, but the aim of applying make-up has always been the same: to look sexy. Or, at the very least, to look slightly less unsexy.

There are two reasons why make-up trends fall out of fashion. The first is simply a realization that all the effort has actually left you looking a bit worse than before you started. At some point, the fashion in Ancient Egypt of dying the palms of hands red with henna was deemed utterly pointless, and similarly, the urge Victorian women had to bleach their hands to make them look as white as possible hasn't stayed with us – if anything, we now viciously rail against the idea with an arsenal of fake-tanning products. The battle against facial wrinkles and spots has been fought for centuries: get this anti-pimple recipe from the *Medicamina Faciei Femineae* by Ovid:

> *Make haste and bake pale lupins and windy beans. Of these take six pounds each and grind the whole in the mill. Add thereto white lead and the scum of ruddy nitre and Illyrian iris, which must be kneaded by young and sturdy arms.*

Today we're sold creams containing "silky-peptimines" or "plumpy-hydrides" that haven't required us to knead anything with young and sturdy arms – but in Renaissance times women favoured egg white to conceal skin blemishes and fine lines. This would give an unusual shiny glaze to the skin, the sort you might see on an apple pie – but in order to look less like a pie, women would attempt to draw veins on top of the glaze, thus ending up looking like a pie with veins. Gorgeous.

But it seems unfair to scoff at make-up habits that are five hundred years old when we've employed equally unappealing strategies within living memory. For all Princess Diana's radiant beauty, her application of navy blue eyeliner did her no favours, nor indeed anyone else who attempted to copy her. Overplucking eyebrows will always leave people with a permanent look of bewilderment and surprise on their face. The hours that women spent in the 1980s attempting to "sculpt" their faces by shading them only ever worked in the particular light the make-up was applied in; leave the building and they immediately looked as if they'd tried to colour themselves in. And applying a fake mole to the upper lip (à la Madonna) was as bizarre as wearing spectacles when you didn't need to (see p.114); five hundred years earlier and such behaviour would have seen such women burnt at the stake.

But the most misconceived make-up was the stuff that simply made you unwell. The classic face-whitener of Elizabethan times was a mixture of lead and vinegar, which at best would leave you with a rapidly receding hairline, and at worst would lead to muscle paralysis and death. Today, some make-up products might make your lips "plump up" by irritating them slightly with chemicals, but that's safer than red lipstick containing mercuric sulphide, which left nineteenth-century women with tremors and missing teeth. Dropping deadly nightshade into the eyes might well make them "sparkle", but it could also make you a bit delirious and unsteady. And as recently as the 1930s, women were rendered blind in the USA by applying a thoroughly toxic product called "Lash Lure". We're fortunate today that the worst injury one can sustain while applying make-up is to poke oneself in the eye with a mascara brush.

introduced reinforcements to the "sumptuary laws" that had been around since the time of Edward III. These rules governing who could wear what, and when, were intended to stop poorer people passing themselves off as wealthier than they were, while also encouraging the production of domestic textiles – and Elizabeth's 1571 Statute of Caps for some reason attempted to reverse the marked decline in the woollen cap industry.

People just weren't wearing woollen caps any more (probably because they preferred wearing a nice hat instead) but rather than encourage the cappers to produce a product that people actually wanted to buy and wear, Elizabeth pronounced that everyone over the age of six – except nobility, naturally – had to wear a knitted woollen cap on Sundays, or be fined ten groats. Fortunately, these kind of dictatorial policies were abandoned well before the twentieth century, and we were never required by law to wear shell suits to church (see p.154).

Holding festivals on frozen rivers

However tempting it might be to gingerly step out onto a frozen stretch of water with the aim of emulating either Jayne Torvill or Christopher Dean, the dangers will still be lurking there in the back of your mind. The reason you're stepping gingerly is because a few days earlier it had been liquid rather than solid. And in a few days, or maybe only minutes time, it'll be liquid once again, it won't support your weight, and you'll suddenly be submerged in water that's barely above freezing point. But during the seventeenth century there were a handful of occasions when London's River Thames was frozen solid; Queen Elizabeth I had already been for a speculative walk on the ice back in 1564, but 1608 saw the first frost fair, when businesses opened up on this new expanse of reclaimed land, and Londoners frolicked merrily between its stalls, eating, drinking and sliding about.

One writer described this as "Great Britain's Wonder" and "London's Admiration" – but while the only surviving reports tell of the fun that was had at the frost fairs, they were a health and safety hazard that must have claimed the odd victim. The danger was exacerbated by people who seemed keen to push the ice to its limits by a) roasting a whole boar thereon, forgetting that heat is the one thing guaranteed to compromise the tensile strength of ice, and b) showing off by hauling a several-ton printing press across it. Some people say that the nanny state unnecessarily wraps us in cotton wool, but if there's one thing we've learnt over the years, it's that having a party on an icy river is inadvisable unless you're all wearing inflatable thermal clothing and connected together with lengths of rope.

Bathing once or maybe twice a month, whether you need it or not

The Elizabethan approach to personal hygiene, rather like that of the average seven-year-old boy, was based on what you could get away with rather than what might be required. Owing to some bizarre code of etiquette that must have left the average citizen exuding a rich odour, it was only deemed necessary to wash the parts of the body that were

actually visible to the public – that is, the hands and the face. The rest of the body gently wallowed in its own filth, with particularly foul smells smothered by the application of perfume – but not even Giorgio Beverly Hills (see p.170) would have been up to this Herculean task.

Strangely, this lackadaisical attitude towards cleanliness wasn't extended to clothing; laundry duties were embraced far more enthusiastically than bathing because of the misguided theory of miasmas (see p.35) which stipulated that foul smells emanating from shirts and trousers might spread unpleasant diseases. Quite why the same theory wasn't applied to the foul smells emanating from armpits and groins is anyone's guess, but bathing was generally thought to allow "badness" to enter the body through the pores. It wasn't until we began to embrace the more likely theory of germs as opposed to miasmas that everyone decided to take a much needed bath. Phew.

Desperate attempts by alchemists to extract gold from urine

The bright yellow pigment of our urine is caused by chemical processes deep within the body whose details are, thankfully, beyond the scope of this book. But gold swishing around our digestive system is certainly not responsible. This may seem patently obvious to you or me, having flushed away thousands of gallons of the stuff knowing full well it has zero cash value – but alchemists of the Renaissance were absolutely certain that gold must be in there somewhere. Because it's a goldish colour. A process of reasoning that probably saw them try to make emeralds out of moss, or diamonds out of saliva.

But try as they might, the secret of converting human waste into precious metal never revealed itself, and remains irritatingly elusive to this day, not that anyone bothers looking any longer. However, it wasn't all a completely pointless endeavour: Hennig Brand's endless experiments on flasks brimming with fresh, warm urine did manage to

yield up white phosphorus as a by-product of the quest for gold. But while white phosphorus has been deployed successfully and highly controversially in modern warfare, you can't fashion it into trinkets or use it to become rich beyond your wildest dreams. Of course, if alchemists had turned urine into gold, it would have flooded the market, thus making gold as worthless as, well, urine. At which point they'd have had to start trying to turn earwax into amber, or faeces into topaz instead. Which they would have found equally tricky.

Pretending to be poor in order to elicit sympathy

We've reached a state in the Western world where, fortunately, working tends to be more worthwhile than begging. If someone does ask you for money on the street, you can reasonably assume that they don't really want to be doing what they're doing, and would much rather replace the long, lonely hours of humiliation and the limited cash rewards with a regular wage and a shred more dignity. But in the sixteenth century, pretending to be penniless was a pretty lucrative business. Whether this was because European citizens combined extreme gullibility with excessive generosity isn't entirely clear, but it led to a huge increase in begging – to the point where it had to be made illegal in Britain in 1536.

Previously, you had to have a licence to beg, but the system was open to abuse. Accounts of the time describe how young rogues would wander the streets blubbing, pretending to be helpless orphans in order to "excite public sympathy"; others would pretend to be traders whose businesses had been ruined by fire, or by war or burglary; some would just feign injury with a pair of improvised crutches, or smear themselves with blood and do the old foaming-at-the-mouth-using-a-piece-of-soap trick. And, incredibly, it worked. The English Statute of Artificers stated in the 1560s that everyone was obliged to work and that begging was simply unnecessary: a controversial pronouncement – but by this time public opinion was swaying against beggars, who were now seen more as conniving tricksters than deserving causes. Before long, inflicting a wound to your head in the hope of making some money just wasn't worth the pain.

Using metallic elements in their raw form to fight off disease

Lined up against some of the other remedies that had become fashionable in Tudor times (for example drinking the blood of a black cat's tail, or killing a wild boar with a stone before throwing said stone over your house) you'd have to say that the simple application of silver or mercury ranked as "pretty sensible" on the medical scale of stupidity. The antibacterial properties of silver had long been recognized – the Phoenecians stored perishables in silver bottles to make them last longer, for example – so its later use to disinfect liquids or to treat burns was a pretty good idea, although admittedly a prohibitively expensive one.

Mercury, however, caused a few more problems. Having been erroneously accepted as the standard method of treating syphilis, the rapid spread of the disease across Europe (following an outbreak amongst French troops attacking Naples in 1494) led to thousands of people swallowing the stuff, rubbing it into their skin, injecting it or, most notably, sticking it in a box, putting their head in the same box and lighting a fire underneath in order to inhale the mercurial vapours. The latter was by far the least likely to actually get rid of the syphilis, but ironically also the least likely to kill you through extreme toxicity. Syphilis blessed its victims with a bad enough cocktail of symptoms without adding mercury-induced deformity and death to the mix; these days, it has been firmly established that mercury and medicine don't really mix.

Attempting to amuse oneself using two pins and a hat

The games and activities that amuse one generation of kids are inevitably looked at with scorn and derision by the next. Just as children of the future will have scant interest in GoGo's Crazy Bones or Catcha Beast, you tend not to find the youth of today arguing over possession of Beanie Babies (see p.179), thrashing away at a whip and top, suggesting a quick game of Buckaroo or asking each other "What's the time, Mr Wolf?"

But as those parents who have watched their children playing excitedly with the cardboard box that once contained a games console will testify, fun can often be found in the unlikeliest of places. And in Renaissance Britain, that fun was derived from two pins – and the action was so compelling that children were still playing push-pin a couple of hundred years later. Philosopher Jeremy Bentham wrote in the late eighteenth century that "the game of push-pin is of equal value with the arts and sciences of music and poetry … Everybody can play at push-pin; poetry and music are relished only by a few." This is probably rewarding push-pin with greater praise than it actually deserves; if you fancy recreating it at home, put a hat on the floor, put two pins on the hat, and take it in turns to knock the hat until the two pins are crossing. If you manage it, you win. It's perhaps surprising that Bentham didn't go on to say "But then again, push-pin is boring, requires virtually no skill and doesn't even give the participants any exercise" – but he probably had better things to be writing about.

Teetering around on a pair of chopines, the Renaissance platform shoe

We normally associate the platform shoe with the 1970s, when the act of strapping on a pair and walking with trepidation down the high street was more an act of mild rebellion than an attempt to make yourself look taller than you actually were. You didn't achieve a higher social status by wearing more enormous platforms – in fact, probably the opposite; wearing bigger platforms merely meant that you were a bigger fan of Gary Glitter (see p.35) or maybe even Gary Glitter yourself.

But the first surge in popularity of the platform shoe was in Renaissance Europe, where women chose to interpret height as an indication of social superiority – and as with the ruff (see p.133) things got a bit out of hand. Some of these "chopines" were as much as twenty inches high, and while this may have given the wearer a fleeting boost to their self-image, this would have quickly evaporated when they had to start moving. Two servants were generally required to assist with getting the things on, and at least one of them would have to hang around to act as a leaning post while the woman made her tortuously unstable way down the street. One writer of the time posited that they must have been invented by "jealous husbands who hoped that … it would make illicit liaisons difficult"; another, Thomas Coryate, pronounced that chopines were "so uncomely a thing, that it is a pity this foolish custom is not clean banished". Laws didn't need to be passed, however; at some point it was collectively decided that twisted ankles were too much of a price to pay for appearing to be a bit taller, and shoe normality resumed. For the time being.

Accusing pretty much every unusual woman of being a witch

Despite what modern-day self-styled witches might like to announce proudly on their business cards, there's no such thing as witchcraft. But this enlightened idea hadn't yet occurred to the vast majority of Europeans in the fifteenth and sixteenth centuries, who would tend to lay the blame for any mishap – be it disease, drought or accidentally shutting your arm in a door – on any random local woman who might exhibit signs of being a bit witchy. Woe betide you if you kept yourself to yourself, or had some kind of visible birthmark, or owned a cat, or were prone to laughing manically for no apparent reason; because rather like trial by ordeal (see p.58) once someone had accused you of being a witch, that was pretty much the end.

Encouraged by the papacy – and particularly Pope Innocent VIII – witch hunting quickly escalated into mass hysteria, with millions of God-fearing citizens becoming incredibly worried that this non-existent coven of evil women were about to overthrow Christianity. In 1541 witchcraft was made punishable by death in England, with the laws tightened further by Elizabeth I in 1563 and James I in 1604; crucially, the new laws left the witch's belongings to the crown, which made local officials incredibly keen to slaughter as many funny-looking but perfectly innocent women as possible. If they couldn't find a damning birthmark on the woman, they'd claim that she'd made it invisible. If the woman exhibited any kind of fear during interrogation, she was definitely a witch, while if she remained stoic and unflinching, that meant she was a witch, too. It wasn't until 1735 that George II made a crucial modification to the law, making it an offence for anyone to *pretend* to be a witch. Because witches didn't exist. This didn't help the thousands of non-witches who had already been needlessly slaughtered by paranoid conspiracy theorists, but better late than never.

Look at a freak, or play hide-and-seek: 1650–1900

It's a two-hundred-and-fifty-year period during which so many profound changes happened in the Western world that it seems almost insulting to lump it all together. At the beginning of it, England was embroiled in a civil war which would eventually establish the way the country would be governed up to the present day, and similar upheavals would subsequently take place across Europe – most notably at the hand of Napoleon Bonaparte. In fact, take it as read that brutal wars were being fought constantly, everywhere, between groups of people over something or other; a gross simplification, sure, but it allows us to ponder the positives – such as the abolition of slavery, the establishment of some kind of social justice, and, of course, the Industrial Revolution.

This last development wasn't to everyone's tastes – not least the children who were forced to work down mineshafts, or the Luddites whose job losses caused them to violently set about new-fangled machinery with sticks and axes. But it resulted in an incredible harnessing of the world's resources, helped to establish great cities, and stopped us once and for all from having to thresh grain by bashing it on the floor. In general we became more healthy, more worldly – even more Romantic. But this didn't stop us, say, placing bets on how many rats in a sack could be killed by a dog in a minute, or injecting our faces with wax as a precursor to Botox. Would we never learn?

Being terrified of what might happen to you if you masturbated

It's a cheap, accessible and hugely popular leisure activity amongst humans of all creeds and colours, but its perpetual association with guilt and shame means that you rarely see people happily masturbating at bus stops, in libraries or at family barbecues. Of course, that's for the best for all kinds of reasons – but for many centuries there was a concerted effort to get people to stop doing it in private, too, by feeding them a whole heap of untruths about the consequences of their actions. Pamphlets and books doing the rounds in Britain and Europe in the eighteenth century described the heinous act as one of "self-pollution", which would not only scar you mentally but also lead to a loss of strength, memory and, indeed, vision.

Victorian conservatism saw boys' trouser pockets aligned to prevent secretive fiddling, while girls were dissuaded from riding horses or bicycles lest they experience any slightly pleasurable sensations. Even by the turn of the twentieth century, John Harvey Kellogg – the eccentric American inventor of cornflakes – was still describing masturbation as worse than the plague, war or smallpox, and many followed his advice that compulsive masturbators be treated with bland diets, the tying of their hands, and even electric shock therapy. Before secretly retiring to a private room and cracking off a quick one.

Making paper impressions of brass plaques

From the thirteenth to the sixteenth centuries, it became fashionable in Europe to commemorate someone's life by having a monumental brass commissioned that might feature them and their families going about their everyday business, and would be kept by the church to serve as a memorial. In Europe, most of these were destroyed during the Lutheran Reformation, but in Britain some four thousand of them survived as a peculiar historical record, giving us an indication of costume and habits of not just the nobility but also the emerging middle classes.

But simply going to have a look at these brasses wasn't enough for Victorian historians; they wished to imprint them in their memory by making a copy on paper using a ball of coloured wax to make a rubbing. And for some reason, this hobby quickly caught on, to the extent that the numbers of people queuing outside churches in the hope of taking away a waxy facsimile forced vicars to start levying a small charge for the privilege. It ticked many of the boxes for a wildly popular hobby – it didn't require exceptional skill, you could compare your collections with other people, and it didn't break the bank. But it was also deadly dull, and doomed to be replaced by racier pastimes. The last brass-rubbing centre in Cambridge finally closed its doors in December 2000, leaving the few remaining brass rubbers to mourn the passing of a golden, if slightly boring, age.

Relating the lumps on your skull to the likelihood of marrying the farmer's daughter

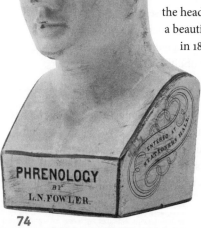

We've seen attempts to predict people's destinies using patterns of bird flight (see p.39) and sand (see p.27) but by the late eighteenth century a comparatively logical decision had been made to focus on individuals themselves and see whether they might yield up any clues. A chap by the name of Franz Joseph Gall had begun to realize that mental activity took place entirely within the head, and he presented his findings in a beautifully titled book, finally published in 1819: *The Anatomy and Physiology of the Nervous System in General, and of the Brain in Particular, with Observations upon the possibility of ascertaining the several Intellectual and Moral Dispositions of Man and Animal, by the configuration of their Heads.*

PHRENOLOGY
BY
L.N. FOWLER.

He was correct in judging the brain to be crucial to the process of thought, but he unfortunately became side-tracked by inventing a bizarre pseudo-science called phrenology, where bumps on the skull could be interpreted as having profound meaning. One raised part of the skull might reveal a flair for poetry, another for vanity, another for the likelihood that you'd knife your neighbour over a trivial argument; Franz's theories were never widely accepted by academics, but many laymen were persuaded by the idea. They rushed to have their heads felt and their fortunes told, despite the fact that it was as pointless as having their kneecap examined, or the contents of their pocket, or indeed a complete stranger's pocket.

Boarding up the windows of your house in order to avoid tax

The combined effects of war, mismanaged finances and general economic uselessness had forced Britain into a bit of a tight corner by the end of the seventeenth century and, as is normal in these kind of situations, the ruling classes looked to impoverished citizens to help them out of the crisis. Wary of imposing a flat per-head tax that had caused all kinds of problems in the 1300s and would do so again in 1990 (see p.177), the idea of a progressive tax was floated, where the wealthy would pay a little more. But the government had no easy way of determining how much individuals earned, and the population found the idea of disclosing this information to be a gross violation of privacy. So the 1696 Act of Making Good the Deficiency of the Clipped Money got around the problem by taxing people according to the number of windows in their house. The more windows, the bigger the house, and the more likely that they were able to pay. In theory.

Of course, the window tax was as unpopular as an income tax – not least because some windows are simply bigger than others. People did all they could to avoid it; if their house had six windows, they'd have to cough up, so they removed the sixth window. Similarly, thresholds of payment at ten and twenty windows were neatly avoided by bricking up more windows. "A tax on light and air", howled those who had plunged themselves into darkness on a matter of principle; today, of course, our earnings are all disclosed to the government, which may be an intrusion into our private lives, but at least we don't have to wander around our homes in semi-darkness.

Drinking beer for breakfast, and encouraging your children to do the same

If you're someone who enjoys having a beer with your morning cereal, it would probably be a good idea for you to put down this book and stagger your way to the nearest doctor, who will probably advise you to replace that early-morning lager with something a bit less potent. But while drinking beer first thing would inject a note of unpredictability into a twenty-first-century working day, in the days of poor sanitation – which covers the vast majority of European history – beer was by far the safest option, because brewing it involved boiling it. Which meant destroying the bugs that would have had water drinkers boarding the bad ship cholera.

Of course, this wasn't the super-strength high-octane lager that turns British town centres into no-go areas after a certain point on a Friday night. This was low-alcohol "small beer" – a phrase that has come to mean something of little importance, but back then was pretty essential in keeping people hydrated without giving them unpleasant digestive disorders. Many employers gave their workers a dozen or so pints of beer for free each day to keep them reasonably healthy and happy, and it was the drink of choice on the breakfast, lunch and dinner tables – again, not for its flavour, but just because it wouldn't do you any damage. Come the advent of clean water in cities, we did well to avoid scenarios where children might be tempted to drink alcohol – until the arrival of alcopops (see p.186).

Going for a ride on a penny farthing

The precursor of the bicycle, the pedal-less velocipede, had two wheels of the same size. Today's state-of-the-art titanium-framed bikes stick with the same concept. But for a brief period in the mid-to-late 1800s, the high bicycle – or penny farthing – with its combination of colossal front wheel and tiny rear wheel, was deemed to be a magnificent idea, and potentially the future of transportation.

It wasn't. You can see how it came about; cycling innovators hadn't yet grasped the idea of gears, so a single revolution of the pedals had to correspond to a single revolution of the wheel it was controlling. A bigger wheel meant more distance travelled, and thus a faster speed.

But at what cost? As the rider was unable to touch the ground with his feet, sudden stops would invariably unseat him – often causing injury – and even gentle stops would require him to dismount and go through the precarious process of getting back on the thing. Was it really worth it? Vigorous, thrusting young speed freaks of the time certainly thought so, and embraced the penny farthing as a means of showing off – the speedway or stock-car racing of its day. Everyone else decided to wait for something safer to be invented – which it was, in 1885: the first geared two-wheeler called, perhaps appropriately, the safety bicycle.

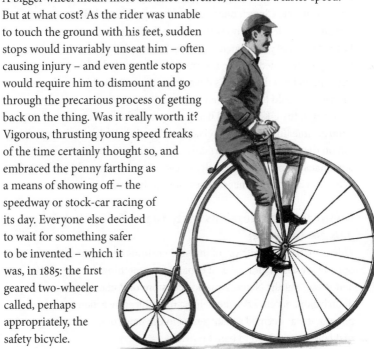

Forcing children to write with their right hand

When things go wrong, we look around for someone else to blame – and while suspicion traditionally fell on women who looked a bit witchy (see p.75) left-handed people have also spent centuries defending themselves against accusations of bringing bad luck. Even today we might double-take if we see someone writing, stirring a cake mixture or conducting an orchestra with their left hand, so it's clearly something that's deeply ingrained in our psyche. There are unpleasant linguistic associations with the word left in many languages, from Latin (sinister comes from *sinistre* meaning left) through German, Norwegian, Spanish, Welsh and Mandarin Chinese, to English expressions such as "to have two left feet". As the Catholic Church once equated being left-handed with being a servant of the devil, it's no surprise that during god-fearing periods of European history, tendencies towards left-handed writing in children were quickly reined in. The favoured Victorian method was to tie the left hand behind the back, as if writing was some kind of involuntary spasm that could be controlled by force. But even as late as the 1980s, children in the UK were still being encouraged to write with their right hands; while this switch conceivably reduced their chances of smudging ink on the page, it almost certainly impeded their academic progress. Fortunately, famous lefties such as Lewis Carroll, Albert Einstein and Winston Churchill managed, somehow, to beat the Victorian system.

Giving your possessions away to prove how wealthy you are (or were)

This book has steered clear of unusual customs and leisure pursuits outside Western culture, lest it expand to something the size of *War and Peace*. But the Native American custom of Potlatch seems worthy of inclusion, because despite being a magnificently generous, selfless pursuit, it was deemed so dangerous to the new colonial economy that laws were passed to ban it outright.

Potlatch involved giving away and redistributing one's possessions. Instead of one's wealth being measured – as it is today – by how many material goods you own, how big your car is or indeed how many windows your house has (see p.69) the indigenous people of North America believed that it was more to do with how much you gave away, so your standing in society was measured by your generosity. While a beautiful idea, the implications for an economy based on accumulating loads of stuff were profound; it made a mockery of possession, made ideas such as competition completely meaningless – and not only did the white colonials think it was stupid, they saw it as a barrier to the locals becoming civilized, and handed out two-to-six-month jail sentences to dissuade them. Today, we still see over-generosity as a suspicious activity that might be worth reporting to the police, but some groups of Native Americans are trying to revive and preserve Potlatch as a utopian idea for the twnty-first-century.

Playing absurdly pointless parlour games such as "Are You There Moriarty?"

If you added up all the time you spent in one year watching bad television, disappointing films, aimlessly browsing the Internet or playing endless games of solitaire on your PC, it would be a statistic capable of inducing a short-lived bout of depression. But all those activities look preferable to an evening of Victorian parlour games, which is what the upper-class Britons of the nineteenth century were forced to turn to when all books had been read, all topics of conversation exhausted, and days began to lapse into extreme tedium.

These were not frenetic diversions, they required little skill and precious little strategy. Many of them required the participants to be blindfolded before they stumbled around the living room attempting to find something or somebody; a classic of the genre was "Are You There Moriarty?", where you would blindly attempt to hit each other

Hairstyles that didn't really make much sense

The ability to style our hair is a wonderful gift, allowing us to improve our appearance with nothing more than a pair of scissors and the cost of hiring a trained professional. (That's partly why it's so heartbreaking for men when they start going thin on top; there's only thing you can do with a bald head, and that's to mournfully gaze at it.) But some of our forebears seized the opportunity presented by a thick, unruly mane of hair, and just, well, made things worse. Sure, there are always going to be hairstyles that we look back on and giggle at with either affection or derision: the 1920s Marcel wave, the Rod Stewart-style feather cut, the much-mocked (but still, for some reason, much-loved by East German men) catastrophe known as the mullet. But these are just styles ebbing in and out of fashion. More interesting are two overlapping strands of misguided hair design: 1) those that require so much preparation that several hours need to be set aside to get ready – hours that might be better spent learning Spanish or building a patio – and 2) those whose construction is so precarious that they're destined to collapse the moment you leave the building.

The latter group are particularly tragic. We tend to assume that when we arrive somewhere, we'll look roughly the same as we did the last time we looked in a mirror. But a hairstyle like the 1970s mohican only required some light drizzle to transform its hardcore punk aesthetic into an embarrassing pensioner's comb-over. Any haircuts that attempt to defy gravity are similarly doomed by physics and chemistry – from the 1960s beehive, to the colossal, layered edifices of the 1980s which, by "getting as much air in there as possible", tended to resemble gigantic meringues. Both could be demolished by inclement weather, or just one inconsiderate person who decided to reach out and touch it because they wondered what it felt like. Of course, one could attempt to offset the likelihood of hair collapse by applying copious quantities of "product", and there lies another rich seam of unpleasantness – from the male wet-look achieved in the late nineteenth century by means of various animal fats, to the gels of the 1980s that cemented hair into stiff and incredibly untactile sculptures.

But in terms of putting inappropriate stuff into your hair, the Georgian era came up trumps. A bastardization of the pompadour saw hairstyles in the 1770s and 1780s compete for outrageousness by embedding objects such as birdcages, model boats and shrubbery, in constructions three feet high; popular styles included "the drowned chicken," "the chest of drawers," the mad dog" and "sportsman in the bush." You became a walking exhibit, a talking point that could only be enhanced by hanging snakes from your midriff or strapping a fish tank to your back. Since then, we've sensibly toned down the act of accessorizing hair, although hair extensions have recently received the kind of enthusiasm that was never afforded to the wig, while the scrunchy – in essence a glorified, multicoloured elastic band – eventually ended up being denounced in the TV show *Sex And The City* as an international signifier of no style, sported by people who simply don't know what to do with their hair.

But while we mock those who fuss unduly over their locks, there's also absurdity at the other end of the spectrum – particularly those teenagers of the early 1990s who believed that "if you leave your hair for a few weeks, it starts to clean itself." As many long-suffering partners, friends and relatives will testify, this plan is no more likely to work on your hair than it is in your kitchen. Thankfully, these days, most of us pitch our coiffure somewhere between these two extremes.

with a rolled-up newspaper before wrenching off the blindfold and weeping bitterly in the corner about the meaninglessness of your existence. Never before or since has the pursuit of fun been so static and slightly self-conscious; today, we only resort to such games as a final act of desperation when the electricity has been cut off.

Going to watch freak shows

It's a terrible human trait, but we love looking at people who look weird. We can't help ourselves. In these modern, reasonably enlightened times, we know it's wrong and we feel guilty, but we're compelled to stare anyway, marvelling at the appalling hand that nature can sometimes deal, and giving thanks that we emerged from embryogenesis

comparatively unscathed. So it was only natural that enterprising individuals with access to two-headed babies, three-legged men and four-bearded ladies would attempt to make money out of this fondness for gawping, and in the nineteenth century we flocked to sideshows and dime museums to see "born freaks" (those whose afflictions were natural) and "made freaks" (who had chosen to tattoo themselves or push a bone through their nose in order to turn a quick buck).

It wasn't until the twentieth century that disquiet about such dehumanizing spectacles began to be widely voiced, but by that point P T Barnum had made a mint out of exhibiting the Siamese twins Chang and Eng Bunker, midget General Tom Thumb, and William Johnson aka Zip the Pinhead, who was a perfectly intelligent man but was nevertheless encouraged to sit in a cage while rattling the bars and screaming. Those exhibited by Barnum didn't do badly financially, but others ended up in low-grade travelling freak shows and endured endless abuse. You'd like to think that this kind of thing no longer happens, but cable TV channels still delight in presenting "sympathetic" documentaries of elderly twins joined at the spleen or cubic babies, knowing that we'll grab the opportunity to slip into voyeuristic mode, secure in the knowledge that the subjects can't stare back.

Believing that magnetic fluid might be coursing through your body

Franz Mesmer, as a budding young physician in the mid-eighteenth century, decided to produce his doctoral dissertation on the effect that planets have on human health. With the benefit of hindsight, we could rewrite his dissertation using the words "none to speak of", but Mesmer wasn't to know that, and his rigorous scientific tests led him to believe that creating a "tide" within the body of a patient – by getting them to swallow an iron solution and attaching magnets to them – would somehow heal them of all diseases.

The patient in question miraculously recovered; Mesmer concluded that the magnets hadn't caused this (correct!) but erroneously decided that it was magnetism within his own body that was affecting his patients, and that he had the capacity to heal people simply by performing "magnetic passes" across their body with his hands. Of course, this had no effect whatsoever, and despite his burgeoning fame, the failure of his experiments saw him leave Vienna under something of a cloud and relocate to Paris; but they didn't work there, either, and he left France under a second cloud. His protégés, however, did make a crucial discovery: that the belief in a psychological treatment was crucial to its success, and helped lay the cornerstone of modern psychotherapy. But for some reason, many people still believe in the healing power of magnets, and spend untold sums on bracelets and trinkets that perform no function other than looking a bit shiny.

Selling dangerous levels of addictive drugs under sweet and innocent-sounding names

We tend to be wary of side-effects of prescribed medicines. Ideally, we'd like our complaint to be targeted precisely by a drug, such that it clears up with the minimum of associated drowsiness, cramps, shivering, memory loss or death. But in the nineteenth century, it was important for people to feel that the drug was having an immediate effect, and that need was fulfilled by a range of unsophisticated, somewhat bludgeoning syrups and linctuses whose heady combination of strong narcotics were enough to render people capable of little other than smiling and dribbling.

The manufacturers of these products knew that sticking "morphine" on the bottle might not have mothers rushing to give it to their families, so they called it "Children's Comfort" instead. One ounce of "Mrs. Winslow's Soothing Syrup" contained 65mg of pure morphine; "Jayne's Expectorant" was part opium; "One Day Cough Cure" combined opium with cannabis, while "Dr James' Soothing Syrup" contained the highly active ingredient known as heroin. As far as we know, codeine was never marketed as "Ronald's Relaxing Remedy" or chloroform as "Sleepy-Bye Snore Juice", but it's not outside the realms of possibility. By the early twentieth century, the American Medical Association led a clampdown on these "habit-forming nostrums", and we largely stopped dosing ourselves into oblivion.

Hiring a photographer to take photos of you and the corpse of your recently deceased child

In the years since photography was invented, we've concluded that taking photographs of dead people is probably best left to pathologists, and that mounting such photographs in frames and popping them on the mantelpiece is likely to upset visitors. In the same way that we're intrigued by deformity (see p.82) we're curious to look at images of the dead (you only have to see the popularity of gruesome websites such as rotten.com to realize that) but on the whole we'd rather not be reminded of our own mortality.

However, when photography was first emerging and starting to replace the painted portrait, a photo of the recently deceased was deemed to be an acceptable memento – so much so that the whole family might pose with the corpse; who'd normally be lying with his or her eyes closed, but would occasionally be posed as if still alive. (As if you'd really want to remember someone with a hollow-eyed, lifeless stare and their limbs positioned into a quizzical shrug.) The Victorians were so superstitious about death – they'd cover mirrors in the house of the deceased, unwind the clocks and bar pregnant women from attending funerals – that it's slightly surprising that they'd stick a photograph of a corpse in their parlour along with a lock of hair. But they did – and in enough numbers for a whole museum in Illinois to be devoted to this single, bizarre branch of the art of photography.

Hoping to bask in the positive medical effects of radioactivity

There are, sadly, still many horrific modern examples of medicines being used on human beings without adequate testing. But when Marie Curie discovered radium in 1898, the excitement surrounding its possible medicinal uses led to a surge in people eager to expose themselves to radioactivity as soon as possible. One of the crucial mistakes was made when scientists noted that many hot springs in health spas were mildly radioactive, and decided that it was probably the radioactivity that was causing the health benefits. So the water was bottled and sold as a miraculous new tonic; fortunately for those who bought it, by the time it reached the markets any radioactivity had dissipated. Unfortunately, the same scientists, realizing this, took steps to ensure that patients had a way of ingesting freshly radioactive water – which was, of course, deadly. One chap by the name of Eben Byers finally died in 1932 after drinking more than three bottles of "radiation water" per day, until his jaw fell off.

Most of the radioactive quack health cures such as uranium blankets and radium pendants were pretty benign, but as the twentieth century wore on and scientists closely involved in work on radioactivity began to drop dead (Marie Curie's papers are still sealed in a lead box and deemed too radioactive to handle) we started labelling radioactive stuff with a bright yellow trefoil sign, rather than make a nice drink out of it and sip it during dinner.

Drinking large amounts of gin without being sure of its provenance

In the late seventeenth century, the English government hit upon a fantastic idea in order to boost the price of grain and encourage exports: deregulate the production of gin, and slap large duties on all spirits coming into the country. It didn't take long for the English to develop something of a taste for this local brew, and by 1703 getting legless on copious quantities of gin was already being described as a "fad" – a polite way of saying that a drunken epidemic had seized the country, and one that makes the alcopop era (see p.186) look like an annual dinner dance at a local Presbyterian church.

Realizing that gin production was outstripping beer production by nearly six to one and was causing not only headaches and regret but also disease and death, the government attempted to introduce a law in 1736 to reduce the binge drinking, but by that point the English were so devoted to gin that they chose to riot. Of the fifteen thousand drinking shops in London at that time, half of them sold only gin, and by 1743 the country was drinking, on average, ten litres annually per head of population – although most of that was consumed by the poor, who were being palmed off with a cheeky, tangy mixture of gin, turpentine and sulphuric acid. By the time William Hogarth had painted his famous picture *Gin Lane* which featured a street full of people barely able to stand, the government were bringing in the Sale Of Spirits Act 1750, which finally had the effect of sobering everyone up a bit.

Attempting to communicate with someone across a crowded room by using a fan

Wafting a fan backwards and forwards has been an effective method of cooling down the face for many centuries – and way easier than strapping an ice pack to your forehead or teleporting to Lapland. During the eighteenth century the design of fans became more ornate, with intricately decorated silk or parchment joined by ivory or tortoiseshell sticks, and were used by upper-class ladies not only to move air, but also as something to peek over coquettishly, to intrigue the kind of men who like the kind of women who hide behind a fan.

Fan manufacturers, imagining a burgeoning market of tongue-tied women keen to lure members of the opposite sex, decided to create the "language of the fan" in order to teach women how to communicate with men without talking to them. A closed fan touching the right eye was supposed to mean

"When may I be allowed to see you?", while threatening movements with a closed fan meant "do not be impatient", and holding a fan over the left ear meant "I wish to get rid of you". It was only ever a marketing ploy, however, and women who did attempt to deploy fan language would probably have found themselves repeatedly stabbing their left knee in frustration with a broken fan, which of course meant "I sense that you don't understand me, because you haven't read the marketing blurb from the fan manufacturer". But the myth that fan language was ever widely understood still persists today.

Wearing a dress that didn't allow you to sit down properly

It's difficult to sum up all the ways in which the huge crinoline dress was a less than brilliant idea. Not only did it give the wearer trouble when sitting down, doorways were as unnegotiable as if you were sitting on the back of a Shetland pony, or carrying a canoe sideways. While the skirts were unwieldy, the frame supporting them was very light, so a single gust of wind could transform a garment designed to hide one's modesty into a free-for-all peep show, and while it may have been designed to conceal the bottoms of larger ladies, it did so by making everyone's bottom look colossal.

This wasn't a sudden burst of madness on the part of designers; there had been a predecessor of the crinoline called the farthingale, which similarly relied on a supporting structure to keep the shape of the dress – but it wasn't until the influence of French fashion started to be felt across Europe from around 1810 that the diameter started to increase, peaking at around the six-foot mark. By the mid-nineteenth century, the so-called "rational dress" movement had begun to campaign for simpler attire that wasn't so cumbersome and wasn't so likely to drag you feet first into a nearby threshing machine; and by 1864 the crinolette was the new thing – a sober version of the crinoline that accentuated the bottom, but didn't make you look like a gigantic toilet plunger.

Prohibiting booze, goldfish in the news: 1900–1950

Easily the most puzzling, tragic human act of the first half of the twentieth century was to send around ten million young people to their deaths to fight in World War I – including many who were shot by their own side for simply not being brave enough to hurl themselves into battle and face certain death. Then we did almost the same thing two decades later but on a far greater scale: 25 million military personnel and 47 million civilians failed to see in the New Year in 1946. The United Nations was established in an attempt to prevent anything so terrible ever happening again, but it didn't stop tension rising between the East and West for decades to come (see p.112).

A personal transport revolution began with the mass production of the motor car, although it took several decades and a few thousand deaths on the roads before it was deemed a good idea

to make people pass a test before being allowed to drive one. We saw a flu pandemic, the arrival of the Jazz Age and the prosperity of the Roaring Twenties, followed by the depression of the Thirties. We could suddenly toast our bread in a pop-up machine, zip up our trousers with a revolutionary new fastener, and pop down to a new-fangled movie theatre for the latest in public entertainment. But what wasn't such a good idea?

Transporting the public in aircraft with large balloons full of flammable gas

When the Montgolfier brothers sent two vastly braver but subsequently far less famous men up in their new hot-air balloon over Paris in 1783, the race to conquer the skies was underway. Jean Pierre Blanchard invented a basic means of propulsion and steering with which he managed to float across the English Channel in 1785, while scientist

Jacques Charles had the bright idea of filling balloons with lovely, buoyant hydrogen rather than hot air. As successive airship designs were built, flown and crashed throughout the nineteenth century, hydrogen was generally adopted for having the best "lift", despite being highly flammable and causing a number of catastrophic fires.

Airship fever began in 1900 with the construction of the first airship by the Zeppelin company, the LZ1 (also filled with hydrogen). Any safety improvements tended to concentrate on keeping fire away from the hydrogen rather than finding a way round using thousands of cubic metres of flammable gas, so when German forces attempted to use airships to drop bombs on Britain during World War I, they were effortlessly repelled by incendiary bullets. But at the time, the only effective alternative was helium; the only significant natural resources were beneath the American Great Plains; and the US government was reluctant to let other countries have it – particularly the Germans. So

the Hindenburg, the last Zeppelin to be built, was filled with hydrogen. And its much-publicized crash-and-burn in New Jersey on May 6, 1937 trashed any confidence the flying public had in airships, no matter what gas they might have been filled with.

Writing "Kilroy was here" on walls in unexpected places

It would be wrong to pretend that graffiti is something that has only blighted inner cities since the invention of hip hop and the aerosol can. Prostitutes in Ancient Greece would scratch their contact details onto walls, while the Romans preferred to etch a bit of political rhetoric. But the first mass wave of graffiti was kick-started by an in-joke among US servicemen.

When newly built ships left one particular shipyard in Quincy, Massachusetts, an inspector by the name of James Kilroy would write "Kilroy was here" on riveted sections of the vessel so he could keep track of how many rivets had been put in by his workers during each shift. Unpainted and often hard-to-reach sections of the ship would thus retain his signature, and as servicemen went overseas, they would idly write "Kilroy Was Here" in similarly unexpected places in the hope of raising a laugh from their colleagues. At some point, the public joined in with the game – without having a clue what it all meant – and the long-nosed chap peeping over a wall become the standard accompanying sketch; he became known as Chad in the UK, El Fisgon in Mexico, Józef Tkaczuk in Poland, and Mr Foo in Australia. Kilroy himself never achieved much fame as a result of the graffiti explosion – but slightly more than if he'd merely chalked the word "rivet" instead.

Taking up the clarinet in order to appear more sexually attractive

Performing is about showing off, and by putting yourself on a stage and managing to not be completely awful you instantly become more beguiling, enigmatic and sexually enticing than the person who is working the safety curtain. In fact, the importance of making an audience faintly aroused has seen the music business slide towards a scenario where the music is of marginal importance compared to the shade of lip-gloss worn by the pouting lead vocalist.

But this causes rivalry and tension between the musicians onstage, because none of them want to be loading the equipment out of the venue; they'd rather be exchanging glances, telephone numbers or bodily fluids with someone who'd been staring at them from the front row. And during the swing era of the 1930s, the clarinet player was, albeit briefly, the central focus of that attention. He was the band leader, the equivalent of Elvis, Tom Jones or Bono. It was a fleeting moment in the spotlight for an instrument that Mozart had first championed (in an "OK, you can sit in the back of the orchestra" kind of way) and is now only softly heard in adverts for milk chocolate or feather-soft mattresses. But for a few years, girls wanted clarinettists, and boys wanted to be clarinettists. Come the rock'n'roll era, however, its limitations as a rock posturing instrument became horribly evident, and today clarinettists are no more inherently sexy than upholsterers.

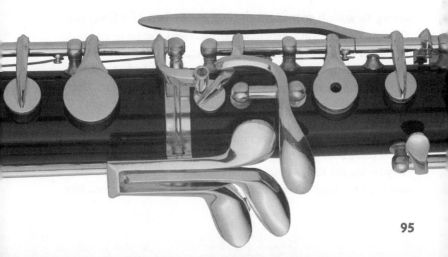

Bouncing up and down repeatedly on pogo sticks

Some fads that involve moderate amounts of exercise such as inline skating (see p.77) or riding a penny farthing (see p.182) have the additional benefit of transporting you from A to B in a shorter time than if you were walking. The pogo stick, however, replaced our carefully evolved bipedal system with a single stick with two foot pads, purely for the purposes of bouncing up and down. You could engineer a certain amount of forward and backward movement (mainly forward) but it was never going to get you to work on time and without injury.

It was patented in 1919 by American George Hansburg, who based his design on an earlier German invention that was made of wood but tended to buckle in high humidity. After he taught the chorus girls of Broadway's Ziegfeld Follies how to use his new, all-metal stick, they incorporated them into a dance routine that established the pogo as the next big thing. But its functional limitations, and the annoyance of trying to speak to somebody when they were using one, saw sales eventually decline. You can still buy them, of course, but they're a niche market – as evidenced by the current availability of a model by the name of Vuertego v3 Stealth, a snip at $349.

Going to watch someone sitting at the top of a flagpole

When American Alvin "Shipwreck" Kelly accepted a wager in 1924 that he couldn't sit on top of a flagpole for an elongated period of time, he'd probably never heard of St Simeon Stylites the Elder, who had perched atop a column some 1500 years earlier for an astonishing 36 years. If he had, he probably wouldn't have taken up the challenge. But he hadn't. So he did.

St Simeon had begun his lengthy residence on high in order to get a bit of peace and tranquility and remove himself from the trials of everyday life, but Kelly's antics started to draw substantial crowds who were eager to squint at a man doing very little at a height of around fifty feet. His first attempt only lasted thirteen hours, but over the next five years various challengers vied with him for the flagpole-sitting crown, and during his 1929 attempt, which lasted 49 days, some twenty thousand people came to have a look. This record was beaten the following year by a Mr Bill Penfield, whose 51-day stint was only interrupted by a thunderstorm – but as the Great Depression started the fad was already waning, with people more interested in getting food on the table than watching someone being a bit of a show-off. We're still ambivalent about the motivations of people such as magician David Blaine who perform public stunts of this kind, and occasionally refer to them as "pole-sitters". Appropriately, the current world record is held by a Pole, Daniel Baraniuk.

Preserving the morals of a nation by banning the sale of alcohol

There's something to be said for alcohol. It's not great for your liver, your brain, or indeed most parts of your body, but in moderation, at judicious moments, it can smooth over all kinds of social barriers. You become more interesting and amusing – or at least you think you do, and if everyone else is drinking they might think so, too. You might not normally want to dance frenetically, but after a couple of glasses of fizz at a wedding the prospect becomes delightful. And without it, most of us would utterly fail to form sexual relationships; we'd just sit at home, looking at the phone and waiting for someone sexy to accidentally call us.

But religious groups in the US, and indeed across parts of Europe, overlooked all these undoubted benefits, and, in the second decade of the twentieth century their campaigns against the corrupting, evil influence of alcohol finally met with some success. Booze was banned in some shape or form by the governments of Russia, Iceland, Hungary, Norway, Finland and the USA over various periods between the two

World Wars, and those who really fancied a drink were forced to get hold of it by either illicitly making it themselves, or finding someone who'd sell it to them under the counter. In the US, mafia groups quickly moved in to fill demand; at the height of Prohibition, ten thousand "speakeasies" were operating in Chicago alone, and the battle against booze was being lost. Franklin D Roosevelt passed the first of the laws repealing the ban in 1933 with the words "I think this would be a good time for a beer". And eventually even some anti-alcohol campaigners admitted that the main effect of Prohibition had been to make people drink more, not less.

Sending hundreds upon hundreds of postcards

The recent explosion in telecommunications technology shows that if you make it easier and quicker for people to communicate, they'll start sending each other notes about anything and everything. Until the 1860s, postal communication was only about long-hand letters, envelopes and stamps; but then John P Charlton filed a US patent for the postcard, a more informal method of telling people what you were up to. Throughout the next few decades they slowly began to catch on, but their popularity was slightly hampered by the fact that you were only legally allowed to write on the side of the postcard which had the picture on. When this law was changed in 1907, postcard mania began. People didn't even care if they had nothing to say, they'd send the postcard anyway. By the end of 1909, a billion postcards a year were being mailed, and in the UK it was a similar story, with millions being popped into postboxes every week.

By the end of the decade, however, some of the novelty had worn off, and German manufacturers – who had previously been exporting millions of postcards to the US – noticed a massive slump. And as alternative ways of staying in touch grew – most notably the telephone – the postcard lost some of its appeal. We loved the erotic French ones from the 1910s, and the saucy British ones from the 1930s, but we lost interest in sending a postcard purely for the sake of sending a postcard, unless we were on a boring holiday.

Attracting attention by swallowing a live goldfish

For a student fad to spread across campus requires only word of mouth, a process that students are notoriously willing to participate in. But for a student fad to spread across an entire country requires the participation of the national press. Today, newspaper reporters are far too busy documenting the lives of reality TV stars or decrying the evils of immigration, but back in 1938 the antics of a potential class president at Harvard were deemed very interesting by the media, and they reported the incident in depth. After accepting a ten-dollar bet, one Lothrop Withington Jr swallowed a live goldfish. That was all. No introductory song or subsequent dance routine. He just swallowed it. And in a classic case of ignoring the parental maxim "Just because he does something

Torture: the only limit is your imagination

The 1948 UN Declaration of Human Rights stated, amongst many other laudable things, that "no one shall be subjected to torture". As long ago as 1798 it had been established by no less a tyrant than Napoleon Bonaparte that torture basically doesn't work; "The wretches say whatever comes into their heads," he said, "and whatever they think one wants to believe." The UN Declaration recognized this, along with the obvious fact that it was deeply unpleasant for those on the receiving end. How splendid it would have been if it had immediately curtailed all global torture – but unfortunately it still occurs in two-thirds of the world's nations, and we continue to exhibit an incredible capacity for creativity when it comes to dreaming up ways of inflicting pain upon fellow human beings.

Of course, we're a bit more squeamish than we used to be; even if we were able to attend a public hanging, drawing and quartering on the streets of London as Samuel Pepys was able to back in the 1660s, most of us would rather stay at home and watch a gentle sitcom on the TV. History is littered with devilish forms of torture that would make the modern stomach turn: the Ancient Greek method of the Brazen Bull involved placing the victim inside a hollow metal sculpture of a bull, lighting a fire underneath and roasting him to death; The Saw, as its name gently hinted, was a bloody medieval punishment consisting of hanging someone upside down and cutting them in half from the genitals to the neck (if not further – by that stage you may as well, after all); while scaphism elongated the torture for as long as two or three weeks, by simply forcing someone to sit, smeared with honey, in their own diarrhoea while they were slowly feasted upon by insects.

Various barbaric methods of impaling, piercing or skewering people to death seem to hold a particular fascination for us today, if not a keenness to give it a try: from the Iron Maiden – a cage which was designed so spikes would slowly and agonizingly drive their way into the body – to oriental variations on the same theme that depended on the quick-growing properties of sharpened bamboo to achieve a similarly gruesome effect. The Judas Cradle (allegedly used by the Spanish Inquisition in the late fifteenth century) involved being sat atop a sharpened pyramid and being forcibly lowered until you divulged any useful nuggets of information, with weights being added to ensure your death when your torturers got bored with your feeble pleading for mercy, while Ivan the Terrible and Vlad the Impaler lived up to their names by using a more straightforward approach – stick the victims at the top of a long spike in a public place and let gravity do the dirty work. This was presumably meant to act as a deterrent to others to commit crime, but people continued to be impaled, so you can only assume that they just really loved impaling. "Oh, our crazy ancestors," we think as we queue up for a visit to Amsterdam's torture museum, but we should remember that as recently as World War II unspeakably painful torture was meted out to Japanese prisoners of war involving bamboo shoots and fingernails. Even thinking about it makes typing this quite difficult.

Modern-day torture has relied on creating maximum emotional and psychological impact while avoiding those tell-tale physical signs that might see the torturer prosecuted. Solitary confinement, mock executions and sensory deprivation are particular favourites, along with the controversial practice of waterboarding; this is debated over endlessly by politicians as to whether or not it actually constitutes torture (it doesn't drown people, it just makes them think that they're drowning) but it's notable that those who deny its capacity to harm haven't actually experienced the horrific practice themselves.

You would have hoped that by the twenty-first century we'd have become civilized enough to properly adopt the UN Declaration and view all torture as a terrible idea – but when that pesky evidence doesn't materialize, it seems that people just have an urge to make someone – and in some cases, anyone – pay horribly.

doesn't mean that you have to", many students copied him.

As it became something of an "intercollegiate sport", records started being set. First three, then six, then a leap to 25, thanks to a Mr Gilbert Hollandersky. By March 1939, new records were being reported in the national press on a daily basis, and students began to see it as an easy way to gain notoriety. (If you see swallowing a few dozen live goldfish as easy, of course.) When the record hit 43, the student responsible was suspended for misconduct, but the all-time record was 210, set by a chap at St Mary's University in Minnesota. A mixture of student boredom with goldfish, objections from animal rights campaigners, and newspapers deciding to concentrate their efforts on reporting the imminent war in Europe saw the fad turn a little sour; goldfish everywhere exercised their gills in a sigh of relief.

Blacking up in order to provide onstage entertainment

There's nothing wrong with getting onstage and pretending to be someone other than yourself. Actors have been doing it for centuries. But there's a point where your powers of impersonation can cross a line of bad taste. Pretending to be a blind person by staggering around with your arms outstretched screaming "I can't see" isn't very realistic, ditto a man playing the part of a woman by wearing enormous comedy breasts and speaking in a high voice. But by far the most inadvisable example from this period was white entertainers painting their faces black, putting on rotten accents and pretending to be happy-go-lucky plantation workers. They never pretended to be oppressed plantation workers whose human rights were being violated – that wouldn't have gone down well in vaudeville – and so depictions ranged from the mocking of a crippled African in Cincinnati ("Jump Jim Crow") to cloyingly sentimental ballads ("Swanee River").

In the early movies, black characters were almost exclusively played by whites who had blacked up, and it reached the absurd point where black actors, singers and comedians who were finally finding mainstream audiences were also painting their faces and lips in "blackface" style. While the American public started to show distaste for the idea of blacking up in the 1930s, the variety TV show *The Black And White Minstrel Show* was still on British screens and using blacked-up actors in the late 1970s. We're much more sensitive now, to a point where even the old Dutch custom of Zwarte Piet (which involves painting the face black but has no racist meaning) just feels very, very wrong.

Wearing exceptionally colourful military uniforms into battle

You don't have to be a master military tactician to understand that the most effective tactic on the field of battle is the element of surprise. Many and various methods have been tried over centuries of conflict to shock and unsettle the enemy – including using elephants (see p.26) – but nothing says "Coo-ee, here we come, boys" like an army wearing bright red trousers and blue overcoats with shiny buttons. Or, indeed, a cavalry wearing plumed helmets and polished breastplates. This, tragically, was how the French army turned up for World War I; the uniforms had effectively been stashed away in a cupboard since the Battle of Waterloo, and, despite them having proved reasonably sensible in previous campaigns they suddenly seemed massively conspicuous in 1914 – almost a request for the enemy to mow them down in cold blood.

This happened almost immediately at the First Battle of the Marne, which saw a quarter of a million French casualties and prompted a more sober choice of clothing for the 1915 slaughtering season. The situation wasn't helped by the army's malfunctioning, ineffective guns; the French government wasn't even able to give them away at the end of the war. These days, the first rule of soldiering is to blend into the background. You might look silly wearing a khaki helmet with a small bush stuck on top, but hey, at least you're not dead.

Pushing a slinky down the stairs

Throughout history, there have only ever been two games that you can play on the stairs. One of those involves having a running race up and down stairs – which, to be honest, isn't something that's restricted exclusively to stairs – and the other is playing with a slinky. Like some of the best inventions, and probably a good proportion of the worst, too, it came about quite by accident: naval engineer Richard James observed the delightful way a spring he was playing with fell off a shelf, uncoiling and recoiling, and discovered that kids quite liked it, too. Seeing a gap in the market for things that look good coiling and recoiling, he and his wife went into business, manufacturing four hundred "slinkies" to be demonstrated at a Philadelphia department store in November 1945; the entire stock sold out, at a dollar a piece, in a mere ninety minutes.

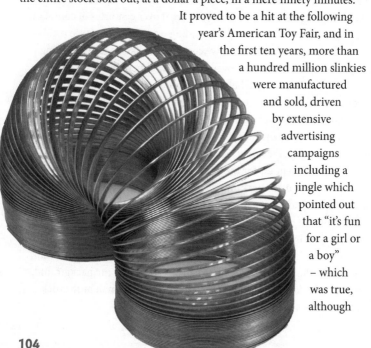

It proved to be a hit at the following year's American Toy Fair, and in the first ten years, more than a hundred million slinkies were manufactured and sold, driven by extensive advertising campaigns including a jingle which pointed out that "it's fun for a girl or a boy" – which was true, although boys were probably a little more enthusiastic. While they've always been lovely, tactile objects, that level of interest was never going to be sustained, and these days they most often appear in science lessons when the teacher uses them to demonstrate the concept of waves. Richard James lost interest, too; in 1960 he apparently left his wife and family to join a cult in Bolivia.

Attempting to contact the dead by using a Ouija board

We're destined to be forever absorbed with the mystery of what might happen to us when we die. Many would argue, with a certain amount of scientific backup, that we simply cease to exist and become incapable of any further sentient thought. More religious-leaning folk might believe that our souls continue to exist on some parallel plane. Others imagine that we spend our time waiting to be contacted by a group of people sitting in a circle with their hands on an upturned glass which has been placed on a board containing letters of the alphabet, and the words "yes" and "no". A bit far-fetched, possibly, but an idea put forward very strongly by spiritualists in the USA during the nineteenth century, who believed that the "talking board" could bring answers from the afterlife.

The first board sold as a "Ouija" was manufactured in 1901, and was quickly copied; by the 1920s it had achieved craze status. From that point on, amateurish séances would be regularly interrupted with the question "Did you move it? No, seriously, did you move it?" To which the answer was always "no", but to which the truthful answer was "yes". American magicians Penn & Teller brilliantly debunked the Ouija board phenomenon with a simple experiment; blindfold the participants, turn the board without them knowing, and watch them move the glass to the areas where "yes" and "no" had previously been. The Ouija board certainly had an effect on people – there's evidence of people becoming mentally disturbed as a result of using one – but it was only ever in the mind, and certainly not zooming in from the hereafter.

Decorating yourself and your home Egyptian-style

Following the discovery of KV62 – better known as the tomb of Tutankhamen – on 4 November, 1922 by Egyptologist Howard Carter, the Western world appeared to go Egypt-mad. Okay, we didn't shave our heads and start wearing wigs on top (see p.13) or start mummifying our nearest and dearest (see p.15) but clothes, jewellery, hairstyles, art, architecture and general nick-nacks all began to take on an undeniably Egyptian flavour. Hieroglyphs, scarabs, lotus flowers and pyramids were suddenly embraced by designers who were keen to exploit our insatiable interest in

the news that was regularly emerging from the Valley of the Kings, while architects were inspired by the clean, geometric lines and started work on buildings with heavy Egyptian influences – including some 69 Egyptian cinemas that were erected in the USA and the UK during the 1920s and 1930s. "Egyptian-ness" was also one of the many influences on the emerging Art Deco movement.

It wasn't all tasteful. You'd find the odd dog-headed statue, for example, and the wearing of gold sandals and heavy eyeliner might have marked you out as a bit over-enthusiastic. But it's safe to say that this was the only time that an archaeological dig inspired a fashion movement. No one went around caking themselves in peat when Tollund Man was discovered in 1950, for example.

Making a crystal garden as a cheap alternative to a real one

Chemistry and entertainment aren't two fields that cross over very often. Perhaps fireworks … although while their production inevitably requires some chemistry know-how, most people aren't interested in what goes into them; all we care about is setting them on fire and watching them explode unimpressively at a height of about forty feet while we sigh in disappointment. But the ability to grow your own crystals in a tankful of water did manage to marginally lift the spirits of Americans embroiled in the misery of the Great Depression in the 1930s. Instead of growing flowers in a real garden (which, if you had one at all, would be used to desperately cultivate vegetables) or buying flowers (which you couldn't afford) you'd look to chemistry to offer you some aesthetic pleasure instead.

They ended up being called "depression gardens" as a result. They were easy to create and didn't require any maintenance – just a few lumps of coal in a tank of water, along with some salt, some ammonia, and either laundry bluing or mercurochrome for a bit of pink or blue colour. Then you just sat back and waited for the crystals to start growing. It probably says something that they were abandoned once the Depression was over – probably because the crystals reminded people of the Depression – and today they're only made by seven-year-old boys from chemistry sets they've got for Christmas. If you wish to be distracted from the current recession, much the same effect can be had from sitting in front of a computer screensaver.

Using an absurdly long cigarette holder

It would be wonderful for smokers if the worst they had to fear was making their fingers a bit discoloured and smelly. But back in the era where doctors would prescribe the evil weed to those of a nervous disposition, or simply to "loosen the chest", cigarettes did indeed appear to pose no more danger than malodorous digits, and for those who worried about such things – particularly ladies of a certain class – cigarette holders provided the perfect solution, and they became fashionable from the mid 1910s onwards.

But as we've seen with shoes (see p.68) and will see again with cars (p.199) once an object becomes a status symbol, everyone wants theirs to be more remarkable than everyone else's. And so cigarette holders became incredibly ornate, beautiful items, made out of tortoiseshell, amber or ivory, and a competition began to try to place the cigarette as far from the fingers as possible. The standard dinner-length cigarette holder was already pretty long (around six inches) but when compared to the excesses of the theatre holder (twelve inches) or the opera (eighteen inches or more) the dinner holder started to look like the model of austerity and restraint. The cigarette holder does still have a whiff of elegance about it, but that's more than offset by the whiff of imminent lung cancer emanating from the cigarette itself.

Hoping that Esperanto might make the world a nicer place to live

While differences in language undoubtedly make the world a richer and more fascinating place to live, and occasionally throw up such magnificent delights as a Chinese toy being labelled with the warning "Do must let children play under the adult", there's no doubt that international misunderstanding has led to innumerable arguments and conflicts that simply weren't necessary. In the late nineteenth century, Ludwik Zamenhof decided that he was going to work towards a utopian ideal where his own constructed language, Esperanto, would become the universal second language of the world, and would help to "foster international understanding". For a doctor and ophthalmologist without a huge amount of money at his disposal he didn't do too badly; in 1905 the first World Congress of Esperanto took place in Boulogne-sur-Mer, and by 1920 a proposal to make Esperanto the working language of the League of Nations was only blocked by the French delegation who were worried about the status of their own language.

As with many wonderful cultural oddities of the era, the expansion of Esperanto throughout Europe was curtailed by the Nazis, who saw its spread as part of an international Jewish conspiracy; many Esperantists were executed as a result. There is a branch of Esperantists which still embraces the idea of *Finvenkismo* or "Final Victory", where everyone in the world will be able to speak Esperanto. But with only an estimated ten thousand people currently having fluency in the language, that ambition is such an uphill struggle as to be almost vertical.

Dressing your children up to look like sailors

The motherly whims of Queen Victoria can be blamed for this long-running and slightly odd habit which continued well into the twentieth century. During a cruise in 1846, her four-year-old son – the future Edward VII – was dressed in a uniform which resembled that of the sailors of the Royal Yacht. This ended up causing something of a sensation which was further fuelled by a popular portrait of the shipmatey royal toddler by painter Franz Winterhalter. Suddenly, any middle-class parent with lofty social ambitions would try to emulate the royal family by sticking their offspring in a blue collar and white bell-bottoms – as absurd as clothing youngsters in a beret and fatigues today. The craze spread like wildfire in America from around 1905 – and remember, this was a nation that was already dressing their children up in the fancy blouses and ruffled collars depicted in the book *Little Lord Fauntleroy*.

The need to incorporate elements of nineteenth century sailor chic into modern fashion has never really died out; you'll see elements of it on the catwalk every decade or so, and middle-class, middle-aged women will still have an urge to clad themselves in blue and white if their schedule takes them within spitting distance of a seagoing vessel. But unless there's an imminent fancy dress party, cladding your offspring in bell-bottoms and a sailor's hat is more or less tantamount to child cruelty.

Concrete blocks and minuscule frocks: The Fifties and Sixties

6

After the restraint, austerity and fear of slaughter that marked the wartime years, you might have expected the Western world to immediately erupt into a frenzy of free love, drug taking and general anarchy. But first we had to deal with the 1950s, a period of repressed social conservatism. Words like "tradition", "values" and "sensible shoes" chimed resonantly with the spirit of the decade, and materialist ambitions coupled with some thoroughly decent behaviour conjure up an anodyne picture of a family with 2.4 children, a nice house, a lovely car and perfectly coiffured hair.

But hair was about to get a whole heap more unruly; rock'n'roll and Beat-generation poetry heralded the emergence of "beatniks" (so-named by journalists to infer an un-Americanness on a par with the Sputnik space missions) who in turn spawned a radical, subversive counterculture. The ensuing excess and flamboyance of the swinging sixties made the previous decade look like a vicar's tea party that didn't even have any cake: as Paul Kantner of Jefferson Airplane was to memorably point out, "If you can remember anything about the sixties, you weren't really there."

Planning your escape from nuclear fallout

The presence of several thousand hurriedly built underground bunkers across the Western world is mainly down to JFK, who not only pondered the possibility of nuclear war in a speech in July 1961, but also suggested that we should think about trying to shelter from it. An old US government pamphlet called "Family Fallout Shelter" – which had hitherto been languishing in some box file – suddenly had to have 22 million copies run off in order to keep up with the subsequent demand; people were understandably keen to protect their families, and if cowering under a table laden with bricks was going to help them, then they wanted to know exactly how to arrange those bricks.

IN THE EVENT OF A
NUCLEAR ATTACK ON THE
BUNKER, GET UNDER YOUR
CANTEEN TABLE FOR YOUR
SAFETY AND PROTECTION

IMPORTANT NOTICE

FOOD IS NOT PERMITTED
TO BE EATEN WHILST
SHELTERING UNDER YOUR
TABLE

Of course, the nuclear strike never happened, and the chances of any cheaply built, leaky underground structure offering any meaningful reduction in exposure to gamma rays was minimal in any case. As the Cold War continued, the billion-dollar nuclear survival industry flourished – but when the Berlin Wall finally came down in 1989, that demand for survival packs and shelters rapidly diminished. We still live under the threat of random terrorist acts and climate change, but protecting ourselves seems so futile that we just tend to keep our fingers crossed instead.

Complaining about how ugly those new Brutalist buildings are

The good thing about concrete is that it's cheap. The bad thing about concrete is that its hulking, grey monotony is so unpleasant to the eye that it manages to pull off the feat of making bricks look almost exciting. This didn't stop architects of the 1950s and 1960s creating grand designs from the stuff, however. Far from it. Many of them saw this austere material as magnificently anti-bourgeois, and perfectly suited to the task of forming dozens of angular post-war buildings.

Sadly, their construction coincided with a period of social and urban decline. If standards of living had soared, then perhaps the failure of the Brutalist blocks to blend in with the surrounding landscape might have been forgiven. But instead, they became inextricably associated with feeling miserable, and came in for stinging criticism that snowballed as the inevitable moss, lichen and damp stains started to remove what little aesthetic appeal the the buldings might initially have had. It took Prince Charles until 1984 to lose his temper at them, labelling a proposed extension to London's National Gallery as a "monstrous carbuncle", but today many surviving Brutalist buildings are viewed as historic monuments that ought to be protected – if only as a reminder of how not to do things.

Pretending to be short-sighted

Wearing glasses isn't that much fun. You have to scrabble around on the bedside table in the morning before you can actually see anything worthwhile. Your vision is impaired as soon as it starts to rain. And in moments of vanity, you wonder whether you'd be more attractive, successful even, if you didn't have to wear them. It seems hard, therefore, to believe that anyone would want to pretend to be suffering from myopia as some kind of fashion statement, any more than they'd want to feign diabetes or leprosy. But in mid-1960s California, that's precisely what happened.

The blame could be laid at the door of various pop stars – Buddy Holly, Roger McGuinn of The Byrds, John Lennon – who had managed the rare achievement of wearing glasses while also garnering screams of appreciation. The thick-rimmed glasses of Clark Kent also helped to portray wearers of specs as perhaps possessing some hidden powers, like the ability to fly through city streets or vanquish evil. Lensless glasses became all the rage as a result, until a marked shift away from student frivolity in the late 1960s saw them discarded into the backs of cupboards. No such luck for those who were actually dependent on them for walking about without repeatedly bumping into things.

Teaching children to read and write by mangling the alphabet

If you spend a few minutes teaching an English speaker the rudiments of the Hungarian phonetic system, you could sit them down in front of a Hungarian book and get them to read aloud from it. Falteringly, sure, and without much feeling for the text, but reading aloud nonetheless. Teach someone elementary English phonetics, however, and the chances of them being able to convincingly pull off a sentence like "the ghost coughed roughly by the lough" would be very slim indeed.

Sir James Pitman, convinced that the many anomalies of written English were badly hindering the development of reading skills, came up with the initial teaching alphabet, or ITA. This collection of 44 sound symbols, based loosely upon our alphabet but enabling consistent spelling, was used from 1961 in many schools to reassure children that reading and writing was logical and reliable, and that curveballs like "foreign" wouldn't suddenly disrupt their learning. But educational purists spluttered as sentences like *"pwt doun thoes traes!"* were chalked up on school blackboards and copied down by five-year olds. The theory was fine: get children feeling more confident about language. But unfortunately, many found the transition from ITA back to proper English incredibly difficult, and nearly all parents found the concept somewhat, er, *confuezing*.

Keeping minuscule Triassic crustaceans as pets

We usually prefer our pets to be more than a centimetre long. Creatures measuring less than this usually find themselves swatted by a newspaper, or squashed under a shoe. But for a while in the early 1960s, people were strangely bewitched by small, larva-like animals suspended in jam jars full of water.

"Brine shrimp" – which is what they are – was a name that would never work for marketing purposes. So, in a triumph of rebranding,

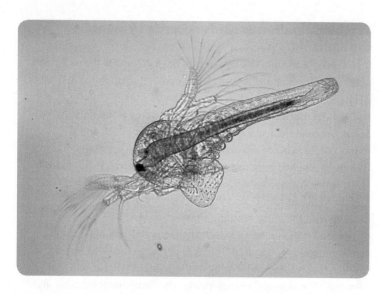

the inventor, Harold von Braunhut, called them Sea-Monkeys, and packaged the tiny eggs (which were in suspended animation, waiting to be diluted) in a gaudy box featuring an anthropomorphic picture of a supposed sea monkey family. The accompanying blurb pushed the boundaries of credibility with such claims as "so full of surprises you can't stop watching them", "they obey your commands", and "they do comical tricks and stunts". Responding to changes in light or heat don't really count as stunts (just observe a cactus over a period of a few weeks, for example) but millions grabbed the unmissable chance to grow their own pet. Incredibly, you can still buy Sea-Monkeys online today, but to get those psychological health benefits associated with keeping pets, you're probably better off sticking with a cat or a dog.

Cramming into enclosed spaces such as telephone boxes for fun

Grown adults foolishly attempted to recreate childhood games of sardines in the late 1950s with the claustrophobic fad of phone-booth stuffing, or telephone-box squash. Sardines worked as a concept because the participants were generally under the age of eight, and thus fairly small; cramming into a cupboard under the stairs while waiting to be found wasn't a test of physical endurance so much as a battle to stop giggling. Intrepid adult phone-booth stuffers, however, can only have been motivated by the possibility of beating an existing record or, more likely, deriving small amounts of sexual pleasure from being in close proximity to strangers.

The world record apparently stands at 25, set by a group in South Africa where, it is said, the practice first originated in 1959. Strict rules having been established (such as there having to be a telephone within the box, that a call has to be either made or received, that the box can't be laid on its side and that the door can be left open but each person has to have half their body within the box) the fad spread to Britain, and eventually North America. The Japanese (who, let's face it, have a competitive advantage through being of slighter build than the average Brit or Yank) failed to join in the craze at the time, but have since made up for it by cramming themselves into Smart Cars in the pursuit of cheap thrills – an even more challenging, some might say pointless endeavour.

Deep-frying chipped potatoes in saucepans full of oil when drunk

There's probably no more dangerous cooking method than deep fat frying, and never more so than in the days before domestic, temperature-controlled fryers, when people would fill a regular pan with oil, heat it to scorching levels, drop something slightly damp in it and watch their kitchen go up in flames. Chips have long been the staple diet of the British, so it's unsurprising that the prospect of eating them has tended to outweigh safety concerns. And after a few beers, when both the lure of the chips and the volatility of the cooking procedure are massively amplified, untold carnage can potentially be caused.

The public seemed to be learning their chip pan skills via a terrifying process of trial and error that, sadly, ended up killing many of them. By the 1970s, television adverts had started to drill into us the correct way to handle chip pans – don't overfill them, keep watching them, and if they do catch fire don't try to put it out with water, as the ensuing wall of flame will probably prevent you from finishing cooking your dinner that night, or indeed any subsequent night. Four thousand people are still injured by hot cooking oil every year, but at least we're slightly more aware of the dangers, and technology gives us a bit of assistance in avoiding those third-degree burns.

Singing "Kum Ba Yah" and actually meaning it

It's something of a sad indictment of our modern cynical society that an inoffensive old song such as "Kum Ba Yah" has lost whatever motivational power it had during the folk revival of the 1960s (when it was associated with the Civil Rights Movement) and is now only used to poke fun at the naïvely optimistic. There isn't actually anything wrong with thinking that the world would be a nicer place if everyone were nice to each other – it's true, after all – but expressing that sentiment via the medium of a gently strummed song is no longer the done thing, unless you want to be labelled a humourless, sandal-wearing hippy.

The Seekers and Joan Baez, both of whom recorded well-known versions of the song, were undoubtedly sandal-wearing hippies – but that kind of thing was positively encouraged at the time, and the song's spirit of unity and compassion was fervently embraced. But the simplicity and repetitiveness that made it so easy to learn quickly made it incredibly banal and irritating – especially when people were trying to get you to join in with it. Fans of Aston Villa football club managed to rehabilitate the song by replacing the words with names of players – "Paul McGrath, my lord, Paul McGrath" – but its failure to prevent 2-0 drubbings at the hands of Birmingham City only underlines the impotence of the spiritual folk song.

Thinking that all colours looked absolutely great in any combination

Sixties counterculture was so awash with psychedelic drugs that it's surprising its participants ever managed to get around to initiating anti-war protests or making backstage arrangements at rock festivals. Depending on how much of the stuff you had ingested, you might get to see bright colours, squares, circles or triangles, rapidly morphing kaleidoscopes or fractals in richly saturated colours with vivid contrasts. But tripping, or the memory of tripping, clearly wasn't sufficient, as a collective decision was made to wear clothing that reminded everyone of what it was like to be tripping.

The process of tie-dying has a long, noble history dating back hundreds of years through various cultures in South America and Southeast Asia. But the way the hippies did it was more a free colour splurge than any faithful observation of traditional tie-dye practices, and the resulting T-shirts resembled a violent altercation in an artist's

Names that you would no longer consider calling your children

When Elizabethan poet Fulke Greville came up with the name Myra at around the end of the sixteenth century, he'd have been surprised and delighted to see that plenty of baby girls were still being given the name some three hundred years later – and that it even experienced something of a post-war surge in popularity during the twentieth century. But when Myra Hindley and Ian Brady were convicted of the Moors Murders in May 1966, the number of girls being named Myra in Britain took something of an inevitable tumble. We want to give our kids names that have positive associations and have some kind of social value; aligning them with mass murderers fails on both counts. The murderous exploits of Thug Behram in India in the early nineteenth century ensured that few if any proud parents would henceforth be issuing a christening invitation to their "lovely little Thug", while the fall of the Nazi regime left Germans with something of a problem, as names such as Adolf, Hermann, Heinrich and many others no longer looked as tempting as they had done a decade previously.

Biblical names have always surged in popularity during periods of religious fervour. Puritans happily gave names such as Hephzibah or Ithamar to their offspring in order to demonstrate their knowledge of obscure passages in the Old Testament, but ensuing generations who weren't quite as God-fearing went for tried and tested options such as John or Mary, while any straggling Ezekiels or Bathshebas got mercilessly teased in the playground. War, regime change and the redrawing of national boundaries also has an effect; prior to the Norman conquest of Britain in 1066, there were plenty of Aelfwines and Aethelbalds knocking about – and even a few Halwendes, despite the name having the profoundly depressing meaning of "lonely". But it only took three or four generations for naming conventions to completely change, and by 1250 our previous compulsion to name children Eadwig and Leofric had been almost entirely replaced with a fondness for William, Henry and Richard.

In modern times we've been so eager for our children not to be mistaken for other children and for them to carve out their own unique niche in the world that we've rushed to saddle them with names that have no historical tradition, and no previous associations – either positive or negative. Instead, they're often just a randomly assembled collection of letters that sound notionally exotic, such as Maxigan, Kaylana or Shailyn (for some reason girls seem to

come off much worse than boys). More worrying is the burgeoning trend of mistaking a child's birth certificate for a sitcom script; Frank Zappa may well have kicked this off in 1967 by naming his daughter Moon Unit, but families worldwide have since shown solidarity with him by choosing names such as Benson and Hedges (for twins), Midnight Chardonnay, Number 16 Bus Shelter, and Violence, while celebrities have exacerbated the trend with such harebrained choices as Lark Song, Audio Science and Jermajesty. In 2008, a New Zealand judge had to pronounce upon the case of a child who wished to change its given name of Talula Does The Hula From Hawaii: "The court," he said, "is profoundly concerned about the very poor judgment which this child's parents have shown." Sadly, we can only sit and wait to find out whether children sporting names like that, or indeed Blue Angel or Legend, will emerge into adulthood unscathed. Here's hoping.

studio. Album cover and poster art also began paying little heed to accepted colour combinations, with the cover of Santana's *Abraxis* being something of a preposterous pinnacle of achievement (and if you haven't seen it, brace yourself.) Of course, as with all counterculture movements, these headache-inducing palettes were eventually adopted by companies trying to sell stuff to young people, at which point said youngsters defiantly started enjoying the colour brown instead (see p.136).

Watching films through light drizzle in a chilly motor car

In the days long before widescreen home cinema systems with 5.1 surround sound, the ultimate family film-viewing experience involved sitting in a battered Ford Zephyr on a remote patch of waste ground, watching images being projected on a large white wall while your kids bickered on the back seat. This offered you a certain amount of privacy – you didn't have to listen to anyone else's kids bickering, for one thing – but wasn't the most luxurious setting you could hope for; drive-ins may have emphasized how you'd be in "the comfort of your own car", but that presupposed a great deal about the interior of the average post-war vehicle.

A chap called Richard Hollingshead invented the concept back in the 1930s, and hurriedly rushed through a patent for his scheme. Success was limited, but after the patent was suddenly revoked in 1950 the number of drive-ins across the US suddenly boomed – especially in rural areas where movie theatres were thin on the ground and babysitters hard to come by. But the combined effects of the increasing price of land and the advent of the VCR spelled the end of the drive-in movie – save for the odd nostalgia-fuelled restaging, or some kind of guerrilla art happening. Home viewing was the future, and brought with it the benefit of not having to smuggle freeloading friends to the screening in the boot of one's car.

Trying to deploy an Aboriginal weapon in the park

The boomerang has only one unique selling point: when you throw it into the air, it's supposed to return to your outstretched hand. This marketing strategy saw an Australian entrepreneur by the name of Jackie Byham shift five thousand of them during the summer Olympics in Melbourne in 1956, and by the late 1950s it had been successfully exported to the US and UK. Entranced by the idea of a stick with a homing instinct, people rushed to buy one – but then encountered the problems that would probably see it rejected by any enterprising toy company operating today.

Firstly, you need to find a piece of open ground where throwing the thing won't accidentally maim or injure an innocent passer-by – it was originally a weapon, after all. Secondly, it's a lonely pursuit; you don't want someone else to catch it after you've thrown it, because that defeats the whole object. Lastly, mastering the art of successfully throwing it is so fraught with problems – wind speed, obstacles, your own pathetic incompetence – that it quickly becomes frustrating. British comic Charlie Drake struck a chord on both sides of the Atlantic with his 1961 hit "My Boomerang Won't Come Back", which described an Aborigine who "waved the thing all over the place" but still couldn't get it to work. Nor could most people. Tellingly, the world distance record for throwing any object – 427.2m – was a boomerang that, crucially, didn't come back either.

Hosting a Tupperware party

If someone asks you over to their house for a social occasion, you'd hope that their invitation wasn't predicated upon you handing over a wad of cash to the host or hostess of the party before you were allowed to leave. Party plan marketing for products such as Tupperware, however, worked on exactly this principle. Sales drives masquerading as social events didn't seem to offend women of the 1950s, who grasped the opportunity to socialize and empower themselves simultaneously, and celebrated the power of female friendship to make a few extra bucks. These days, socially over-sensitive nations such as the British no longer much care for the idea of their mates making commission out of persuading them of the merits of a set of plastic bowls – although, strangely, it still seems to work for sex toys.

But Tupperware parties still drive multimillion pound businesses in countries such as Germany, Australia and New Zealand, where people seemingly don't mind setting aside a couple of hours to attend a living, breathing, real-time advertising campaign – thus disproving the old maxim that you should never mix business with pleasure.

Becoming skilled at hula-hooping

The hula-hoop craze also started in Australia, but its origins were slightly more frivolous than that of the boomerang; it simply allowed people to gyrate their hips repetitively in order to keep a hoop revolving around their waist. That's all there was to it. No deeper levels of cultural meaning; it wasn't an elaborate courtship ritual or a method of destroying one's prey. But once you'd learned how to do it, all you could really do was keep doing it in a bizarre test of personal endurance, or, indeed, patience. Nevertheless, when they were first launched in 1958 in the USA, 2.5 million were sold in a mere two months, and for the next eighteen months stores continued to be swamped with people seeking plastic hoops.

The problem that the manufacturers had subsequently was to get people to believe that there was any point in persisting with hula-hooping. Sure, there are marginal health benefits, but the key was to persuade people to try to outdo each other in the hula-hooping stakes, either by doing it for longer than anyone else, or keeping thirty of them going at once, or doing a tasteful hoop-based dance routine to the sound of Herman's Hermits. So an annual competition was introduced in the USA in the 1960s to try to keep hula-hooping alive; it continued until 1981, by which point it had been made to look a bit static and tame by other leisure pursuits such as skateboarding, abseiling and gunrunning.

Battling depression with psychedelic drugs

Swiss chemist Albert Hoffman discovered the psychedelic effects of LSD in April 1943, after an experiment that saw him reach a state of acute anxiety, terrified that his body had been possessed by a demon. Rather than quietly dispose of the substance, and based on this evidence that its use might make people think that their bodies had been possessed by demons, Hoffman's employers, Sandoz Laboratories, instead distributed huge quantities to researchers into psychotherapy during the 1950s.

They were advised to have a go with it themselves, to get a feel for its effects – but the problem with LSD was (and is) that these effects could differ wildly for different people, or even differ wildly for the same person on two different occasions. This made testing the drug under controlled

125

conditions incredibly difficult, and while it was claimed that there were beneficial effects in the treatment of alcoholism and certain kinds of depression, research stopped in the mid 1960s when the US government, fearful of LSD's fashionability among young people, began to introduce measures to curtail its use. Sandoz stopped producing LSD in 1965, and by 1970 the US government classed it alongside heroin as having "no medicinal value". This is still disputed by a few medical professionals, but they're generally ignored, perhaps out of fear that they're off their heads on psychedelic drugs.

Wearing miniskirts because there was no other option

Towards the end of the 1950s, the conservative world of contemporary women's fashion suddenly started to create the odd provocative, risqué look. However, some of us just aren't suited to provocative looks, and any attempts we might make to try them out aren't so much risqué as downright risky. Short shorts, which didn't leave much of one's bottom to anyone's imagination, started making an appearance in around 1957, but the choice of whether to wear them or not was still very much up to the individual. The crucial change in the 1960s was down to the colossal popularity of the miniskirt; by 1967 clothes manufacturers seemed to have made a collective decision that it was going to be the only kind of skirt available on the British high street for young women.

So, rather than sport fashions that were five years out of date or sweat over a sewing machine to make their own, more modest clothes, women reluctantly adopted the miniskirt across the board. While some saw it as a "tool of rebellion" and enjoyed using it to flaunt their sexuality, others nervously tugged at their hemlines while waiting patiently for the 1970s, when a feminist reaction against the objectification of women finally saw skirts lengthening again. Of course, we still wear things that are hideously unsuited to us from time to time – but that's more on account of our own poor taste than the lack of any alternative.

Casually wielding a yo-yo

Over the years, the popularity of yo-yos has gone up and down as regularly and rapidly as yo-yos themselves. While there's evidence that they've been around since ancient times, the modern story begins in the 1920s, when a Filipino gentleman by the name of Pedro Flores started manufacturing the "yo-yo" (a Tagalog word meaning "come back") in California. It's often suggested that the yo-yo was originally a weapon, but this does tend to conjure up images of jungle dwellers doing spectacular yo-yo tricks to render animals unconscious, when what they actually did was chuck a stone with a cord attached to enable easy retrieval.

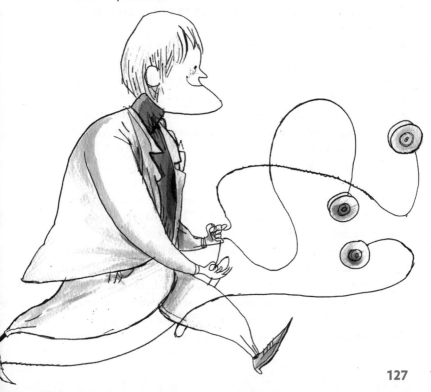

Yo-yos steadily increased in popularity throughout the middle part of the twentieth century, but it was a television advertising campaign in 1962 that suddenly had everyone yo-yoing, with 45 million units sold by the end of that year. Unfortunately for the manufacturer, Duncan Toys, the passing of the word yo-yo into common parlance saw them lose the rights to the trademark in 1965, and a yo-yo free-for-all began. Since then, the toy has fallen into roughly five-year cycles of popularity, partly enforced by toy manufacturers who know that while trying to continually market the toy is pointless, after five years the general public will have forgotten the yo-yo's limitations as a source of entertainment.

Putting on a pair of cardboard specs to experience a 3D movie

The early 1920s was an astonishing period for innovation in film. Jaws were dropping at the first experiments with synchronized sound, Technicolor films had started to receive nationwide distribution, and a 3D film, *The Power Of Love*, was screened in Los Angeles in 1922 to a roomful of people wearing spectacles with one green and one red lens. Tricking each individual eye into seeing separate images to create a 3D effect wasn't new, but enabling a roomful of people to experience it together was expected to revolutionize cinema.

It didn't, of course – although enthusiasts continued to dedicate themselves to the form, and the development of Polaroid filters paved the way for what's known as 3D's "golden era" between 1952 and 1955. It was heralded by *Bwana Devil*, a 3D film with the enticing tagline "A lion in your lap! A lover in your arms!" (Given the choice, one would probably plump for the lover.) One review ended: "The worst movie in my rather faltering memory … I immediately went to see a 2D movie for relief." Nevertheless, it was followed by a series of more critically acclaimed 3D-ers such as *It Came From Outer Space*, and the future of the medium for a while looked rosy. Unfortunately, the need to project two prints, the difficulty of keeping the two in sync without giving your audience vicious migraines, and the problem of people at the sides of the cinema not being able to experience the full effect meant that 3D went into decline. Today, we're so urbane and sophisticated that we consider an alien's head magically emerging from a 2D surface to be, well, a bit gimmicky.

Sharing all your possessions with a bunch of strangers while living in a jerry-built shack

Sharing one's living space is fraught with problems. If you're cohabiting with someone who allows you to interfere with them sexually, it makes their appalling habits (such as leaving toenail clippings on the sofa and milk out of the fridge) a little easier to bear. But if all that links you together is a desire to have a roof over your head, it's likely that your lives will be regularly shattered by blistering arguments over ownership of shampoo. That's just how it is. And it makes you yearn for some kind of privacy.

Communes, however, appear to have been free of such petty bickering. This 1960s counterculture approach to domesticity, jettisoning the traditional nuclear family and replacing it with a heady mixture of vegetarianism, Eastern philosophy, nudity, group decision-making, free love and the sharing of material goods drew thousands of people out of the rat race and into homes where bean casseroles were as plentiful as self-styled flower-children and psychedelic drugs. These gently hallucinating extended families enthusiastically went "back to the land" while preaching peace and goodwill to all men; what's not quite as widely documented is why these communes slowly began to die out towards the end of the 1960s. Surely it can only have been down to arguments over failing to put the lid back on the toothpaste.

Creating that special mood with a lava lamp

A chance visit to a British country pub saw one Mr Edward Walker discover a bizarre egg timer behind the bar, consisting of a lump of wax suspended in liquid that would melt and rise to the surface when heated. Keen to steal the idea and make some money out of it, he was delighted to discover that its inventor was dead, so after perfecting what he described as a "display device" he filed a patent for it in 1965. At a trade show in Brussels it caught the eye of a couple of Americans who bought the US rights, renamed it the Lava Lamp and started shifting millions of them each year from a factory in Illinois.

Walker retained the rights in the UK, keeping the formula of the lamp's contents a strict secret. And thanks to people who were desperate to make their "pads" more "groovy" he found international success. "If you buy my lamp, you won't need to take drugs," he said, ignoring the fact that many people found drugs and lava lamps to have a perfect synergy. Walker also opined that his invention would "always be popular; it's like the cycle of life." On this count, however, he was very wrong. By 1976 sales had slumped to a miserable two hundred a week, and Walker was probably wondering why he hadn't put more effort into his other great love, naturist parks and nudist films. Fortunately, his lamps found themselves rehabilitated in the 1980s as part of retro chic, and today they're an essential inclusion in any post-ironic sitting room. But for how long?

Immobile pets and King Crimson cassettes:
The Seventies

If you were forced at gunpoint to identify unusual human behaviour associated with the 1970s, you'd probably start by gabbling on about the colossal errors that were perpetrated in the name of fashion; you can look at a photograph of a social event from 1972 and be just as astonished by people's clothing choices as if they were clad in eighteenth-century French court costume. But while horn-rimmed glasses, wing collars, platform shoes, A-line skirts and violently flared trousers are distressing to the modern eye, their influence still occasionally bobs to the surface, like a cigarette butt that refuses to be flushed away.

Other 1970s ideas that seemed fleeting and ephemeral have stuck around even more stubbornly. When the first facelifts were performed they were regarded as a passing fad, but now we're as desperate as ever to go under the knife and make things bigger (or, very occasionally,

131

smaller). Feminist theories that were widely scorned have, thankfully, gained acceptance; men no longer assume that their wife will be cooking dinner every night, although parity of earnings is still, for some reason, maddeningly elusive. And while we no longer "Do The Hustle" or unleash torrents of saliva at the Sex Pistols, the musical influence of both disco and punk is everywhere.

While we struggled with the consequences of oil crises, the continuing Cold War, stagflation and left-wing terrorism, we occupied our conscious and subconscious minds with some of the following (which we embrace few of quite as heartily today).

Protecting toilet rolls from everyday stresses and strains with knitted covers

Some things just don't need protection. Tartan bodywarmers for dogs aren't remotely necessary, and represent something of an indulgence on the part of the dog's owner. The amount of cardboard packaging that envelops, protects and nurtures the average Easter egg on its journey from the supermarket to your home could be described as excessive, especially bearing in mind its eventual destiny. But toilet roll covers must rate as the most needless protective device yet devised.

The number of critical shocks sustained by the household toilet roll during its short life spent in your bathroom are limited to the featherlight settling of dust, and the gentle wafting of air. Neither of these things particularly distress the toilet roll, or indeed impinge upon one's enjoyment of it. These covers came in a range of fanciful animal-like designs, indicating that over-enthusiasm for craft projects was to blame for us being saddled with these useless knitted sheaths that stopped us getting toilet paper off the toilet roll. Which, let's face it, is the point of a toilet roll.

Heating your dinner by boiling it in a plastic bag

Convenience food will be with us for as long as there are people who think that cooking is some kind of black art, a fringe activity that's indulged in by poncy gastronomes with too much time on their hands. But even today's most microwave-dependent citizen would balk at a plastic pouch containing a lump of cod in parsley sauce – and that must surely mark out boil-in-the-bag as a low point of the quick'n'easy meal industry.

Well into the 1970s, the words "boil in the bag" could be casually dropped into an advertising campaign for, say, ready-made curry, without fearing a colossal slump in sales. In fact, quite the opposite: this was the cutting edge of phenomenally lazy cuisine, and we slothfully embraced it. To be fair, the contents of the bag were more dubious than the system itself, which has been rehabilitated by gourmet chefs such as Joël Robuchon and Heston Blumenthal (although understandably they call it *sous-vide* instead) but it has neverthless become synonymous with glutinous, unappetising slop. And the only circumstances under which we'd be prepared to boil food in bags today would either be during a jungle expedition, or a war.

Not being ashamed of being a devoted fan of Gary Glitter

Disgrace is a curious thing. There are many reasons why Gary Glitter could have lost his broad appeal since his 1973 heyday: the overwhelming size of his silver epaulettes; the abundance of clearly visible chest hair; the questionable showmanship; our unwillingness to be told to "come on, come on," by a man staring at us in a maniacal fashion while jabbing a podgy

finger in the air. And that's before we've even got around to analyzing the substance of the music itself.

But the media furore surrounding his possession of child pornography and his subsequent conviction for paedophilia has effectively sealed his back catalogue in a heavy box and dumped it over the side of a ship. Wedding DJs aren't that keen on rounding off their set with "Leader Of The Gang" any more. Advertising companies are reluctant to market products using a Glitterbeat. Gary Glitter fan conventions are noticably thin on the ground. It's even possible that you may never hear him sing again, unless you actually own one of his records and fancy a trip down memory lane. Your neighbours are unlikely to assume that you're a child molester if you listen to it, but maybe best to keep the volume on a low setting.

Covering your floor with shag pile carpet

As the hair on our heads became more unruly, so did our carpets. By the 1970s, the shag pile had reached a length of as much as three

inches, and while this presumably symbolized sophistication and slight decadence, it was instrumental in creating dirt, filth, and untold graft for the poor soul whose task it was to clean the thing.

Whole ecosystems were able to flourish undetected at floor level, kept nourished by fragments of food and the tasty bits from the underside of nail clippings. Now, rugs can be shaken out. You can dangle them out of the window and watch the debris cascade to the ground beneath. Not so with something that's nailed to the floorboards – so the vacuuming of a shag pile was complemented by combing it with a rake-like object. Within a short space of time, your carpet looked more like an explosion in a factory that produced both wool and cheese'n'onion crisps. Our realization of the shag pile's myriad disadvantages sent us fleeing, panic stricken, into the equally aesthetically dubious arms of laminate flooring.

Using mood rings as an emotional compass

Human beings are complex creatures. Several millennia of social interaction have enabled us to assess other people's state of mind, sense awkward situations and react accordingly. But someone in the late 1960s decided that this emotional latticework could be neatly distilled into a colour-coded mood ring. Made out of thermotropic liquid crystal, it reacted to your body heat – or, more precisely, your finger heat – and changed its hue accordingly.

Quite why heat was supposed to signpost mood swings is unclear; after all, not everyone breaks out in hot flushes when they're mildly amused (thank goodness) and while the accompanying mood ring chart might have indicated that someone was "passionate", "harassed" or "overworked", a more accurate chart would have said "going down with mumps" or "competing in the 400m hurdles". Strangely, no fewer than three people – Marvin Wernick, Joshua Reynolds and Robert Parker – lay claim to the invention of this remarkably useless trinket.

Preferring things if they were brown

The kaleidoscopic madness of the 1960s gave way to a more refined, sophisticated approach in the 1970s, with a focus on one particular palette of colours: brown. Things might have occasionally swung green-wards into an olive-type hue, or yellow-wards into ochre territory, but there was an omnipresent brownish tinge. Wearing your brown trousers or brown skirt, you'd put on your brown shoes, open your brown front door and get into your brown car. You'd drive past a few brown shop fronts. Then when you got back home, you'd discover that your furniture and your carpets were still brown. And not even a very nice brown.

But perhaps the apotheosis of this unusual fondness for the beige, the buff, the caramel, the chestnut, was the urge to clad as many rooms as possible with pine panelling. House interiors would look like a Scandinavian sauna at best, and a poorly lit magistrate's court at worst. Sure, it was inexpensive, easy to install and covered up nasty plasterwork, but it left future generations dealing with bouts of depression and gruelling weekends of DIY to put it right.

Playing with toys that were loud, irritating and dangerous

You can't really blame children for wanting a toy whose sole function is to make as much noise as possible. Everyone is born with an inbuilt limit on the number of decibels they're able to generate, and if you're at an age when that limit is a constant source of frustration, the ability to crash through it by spending a few pence is irresistible. Clackers fulfilled that need; they were two rock-hard acrylic balls connected by a piece of string, and if you got the knack you could make these balls smack against each other loudly and repeatedly for hours on end, while you were repeatedly told to "stop that" by anyone older than you.

These balls were presumably tested for strength prior to being sold, but the manufacturers hadn't counted on the ferocity with which they were going to be "clacked". If you really put the effort in, you could get them to shatter explosively; this led to children with damaged wrists through the clacking, and eye injuries from the flying shards of plastic. They were removed from the shelves, then relaunched in tougher material – but when they started (somewhat predictably) being used as nunchaku-style weapons in local schools, parents and teachers had an excuse to call a halt to clacking once and for all. And noise-obsessed children were forced to let off fireworks or take up the trumpet instead.

Making a macramé owl

Many creative hobbies enable you to make something reasonably impressive, or useful, even if your skill set is quite limited. Novice cooks can knock up tasty pasta dishes with minimal guidance. The beginners guide to origami will have you folding a neat-looking butterfly within a couple of hours. Woodworking students should be able to build you a CD rack without losing too many fingers. But anyone embarking on a course of macramé in the 1970s would have given one of two decoratively knotted

presents for Christmas, and neither looked particularly pleasant. One was a device for hanging pot plants from hooks. The second was an owl.

These horrific two-dimensional representations of birds of prey represented the entire scale of ambition for many macramé enthusiasts. Once they'd got the hang of the half hitch and the alternating square knot, they'd make an owl. And then another, slightly different owl. It's not as if macramé is particularly suited to the owl format. The finished item looked more like a badly disfigured table mat. And they frightened small children from walls throughout the Western world. Almost inexplicable.

Going to see highly pretentious music with lofty ambitions performed in a stadium by rock musicians

The masses have never really taken to classical music in a big way. As hummable as portions of *Symphonie Fantastique* might be, Hector Berlioz wasn't the Elvis Presley of his day; the general public were far more interested in traditional folk ditties. And while Stravinsky's *Rite Of Spring* might have caused outrage at the Théâtre des Champs-Élysées in 1913, most people outside that theatre couldn't have cared less.

But for a few years in the early 1970s, high concept, complex music had a bizarre surge in popularity. Impenetrable storylines played out across several sides of vinyl and encased in gatefold sleeves would sell millions of copies, and live reinterpretations of great classical works would be played in front of packed venues – mainly men, granted, but human beings nonetheless. A song lasting twenty minutes or longer didn't cause anyone to bat so much as an eyelid – indeed, if it lasted less than ten minutes, the audience would feel short-changed. Then, as quickly as it had caught on, pseudo-classical rock music became incredibly uncool. Fortunes would never again be made from arranging Bach's *Brandenburg Concerto No.3* for a four-piece rock band.

Buying someone a fondue set: the gift that doesn't keep on giving

Some gifts for the kitchen are certain to languish at the back of the cupboard. The pasta machine, the linchpin of a gruelling procedure that leaves you wondering why you didn't just buy a packet of the dried stuff. The mandolin – an appallingly dangerous implement unless it's put well out of reach of humans. The steamer. The ravioli tray. And the fondue set.

The seventies saw us attempt to embrace this curious Swiss dining habit, because it was supposedly fun, communal and slightly exotic. But it was also curiously unsatisfying. Fondue only came into existence because of the harsh Swiss winters rendering bread stale, and cheese too hard to do anything but melt it down – but we fetishized this peasant meal and turned it into a themed evening. Once. Because fondue is a nightmare: it's messy, it's fraught with issues of etiquette (the double dip, the licking of the fork), it can lead to unpleasant stomach ache if you drink anything cold, and it fails to tick several nutritional boxes. So the gear goes back in the cupboard, in favour of knives, forks, plates, and boil-in-the-bag cod in parsley sauce. Much better.

Breaking down social barriers with a game of *Twister*

While Ideal and MB Games were making games of "nerve and skill" like *Mousetrap* and *Connect 4*, Hasbro brought us *Twister*, a terrifying test of embarrassment thresholds. The adverts showed groups of people squealing with joy as the spinner instructed them to put their right foot on blue, or left hand on yellow, their limbs entwining and bodies interlocking as necessary. Presumably there are millions of uninhibited people who had fun, but many will have been mentally scarred by its use as a social icebreaker.

Office parties could become dramatic scenes of emotional torture, as an unwilling participant would find their head squashed against the

Whatever you do, don't point at rainbows

Sometimes we're blessed with good luck. At other times things go incredibly badly and we end up with our head stuck between some railings. Humankind has always been eager to work out why it is that some people don't get their head stuck between the railings and others do, and it's unlikely that this curiosity will ever dissipate; as a time-saving all-purpose solution, people will continue to offer generic prayers to those celestial beings that supposedly control our destiny, but they'll also be developing incredibly complex rituals of superstitious behaviour in a miserable attempt to micro-manage any runs of bad luck.

For example, we know that ships sometimes sink, and planes sometimes crash. But for some reason, the 1970s saw a fanciful theory from a decade earlier – namely that one particular triangular expanse of ocean between Puerto Rico, Florida and Bermuda was terribly dangerous – take an iron grip on the public imagination. Three books, published between 1969 and 1974, whipped up speculation about its inherent dangers, and had people nervously consulting maps lest their Caribbean cruises venture anywhere near it.

Which they invariably did, because one of the world's busiest shipping lanes passes through it. Nearly all of the ships made it out. Some planes went through it, too. Nearly all of them landed. The ones that didn't were probably victims of unpredictable weather associated with the region, and probably not, as was thought by some, down to malfunctioning technology from the lost city of Atlantis. Insurers researched the phenomenon; they concluded that it was no more dangerous than any other triangle. Barry Manilow, bless him, immortalized it in song. "Bermuda Triangle," he sang, "it makes people disappear. Bermuda Triangle, don't go too near." But steering clear of the Bermuda Triangle was as ludicrous as not going outside because that's where car accidents happen. Few people worry too much about the Bermuda Triangle any more.

Superstition is generally founded on this kind of unscientific analysis of past events, and using that analysis to attempt to explain what'll happen next. In the past, we have believed that if children pick dandelions, they'll wet the bed, and if you put a pair of bellows on a table, there'll be a fight. Now, it's possible – or even certain – that children have wet the bed after picking dandelions, because children sometimes wet the bed, and they sometimes pick dandelions. Similarly, it's statistically probable that fights will have taken place within sight of a pair of bellows and a table, but it's unlikely that the bellows had much to do with it, unless they were a particularly gorgeous pair of bellows whose ownership was subject to a long-running debate.

Here are a few more confused examples of cause and effect that we've embraced in the past: If you sweep under a woman's chair, she'll never marry; if you turn a loaf of bread upside down, there'll be a shipwreck; if you smell your own feet, you won't get cramp; if you close a door that opens by itself, you'll be the first person in the room to die; if you split a sapling in half and pass someone through it, naked, three times at daybreak, it'll help them to recover from their hernia; if you look at mushrooms they'll stop growing; if you get a child to ride on the back of a bear it'll be cured of whooping cough; if you crush an eggshell it'll stop a witch being able to use it as a boat; and so on.

Similarly, while meeting an elephant or shaking the hand of a chimney sweep has been said to be incredibly lucky, the list of activities that has supposedly heralded the arrival of bad news is way, way longer: carrying bees across water; laying eyes upon a white mole; dreaming of shoes; sharing a towel; buying a broom in May; saving the life of a drowning man; cutting your nails on a Friday; picking up a left-handed glove; pointing at rainbows…

It's easy to look back and laugh at any number of these, and wonder what on earth we were thinking. But our descendants will look back at us and scoff at the fact that we still avoid walking under ladders, or pay more attention than necessary to the fact that a black cat has just strolled casually across our path. But by that point, they'll have developed their own equally ludicrous patterns of behaviour, such as never recharging their robot on a Monday. *Plus ça change.*

plastic sheet by the arse of Maureen from the typing pool – only for
her to unpredictably and tragically break wind. *Twister* is now spoken
of with a nudge and a wink as synonymous with swingers' sex parties,
while we've moved on to play games online that don't even require us to
be in the same country, let alone accidentally touch each other's nipples.

Attempting to produce your own simulacrum of commercially available soft drinks

Towards the end of the decade, kids suddenly became wildly excited
about something that had been invented some 75 years earlier, which
is unusual in itself. The "apparatus for aerating liquids" was originally
marketed by gin distillers W & A Gilbey as a luxury item for well-to-do
households who wanted their cold drinks to have that extra pizzazz.
But for some reason it took a few decades for them to identifiy their
target market and have a hit with SodaStream – possibly the only
kitchen gadget that shifted millions of units through pester power.

Children like fizzy drinks. They like them so much that they'll blow
air down a straw in the forlorn hope that it'll carbonate their orange
squash; as we all know, this doesn't work for all kinds of scientific
reasons. SodaStream did work on the bubbles front – but there was
a problem. Kids consume so many cans of fizzy pop that they're virtually
connoisseurs. They know fake Coca-Cola when they taste it. And so
the gadget that they'd yearned for for months gradually lost its appeal,
as we all remembered that there are some things – like cornflakes and
combine harvesters – that it's best not to try making yourself.

Keeping a pet rock

The success story of the Pet Rock in 1975 is even more remarkable
when you consider that people could have made their own for next-to-
nothing. But Gary Dahl somehow persuaded people that his were more
authentic; some five million rocks from Rosarito Beach in Mexico were

given a pair of googly eyes, sold to delighted customers at $3.95 a pop, and given pride of place on mantlepieces everywhere.

It came with a comical manual – "place it on some old newspapers; the rock will never know what the paper is for, and will require no further instructions" – but many people truly loved their rocks. Psychological studies have shown that pets can improve our mental well-being, but the eagerness with which humans anthropomorphized a lump of stone and lavished their affections upon it took Dahl completely by surprise. It also begat a spate of copycat products that desperately tried to sell something dirt cheap and ultimately useless at a massive mark-up, but nothing came close to the profit margins earned by the Pet Rock.

Relieving stress via some primal screaming

Arthur Janov published his first book, *The Primal Scream*, in 1970. He believed that neuroses could be resolved and treated by re-awakening pain that you may have suppressed since childhood, and re-experiencing that pain within a controlled environment. In return for money, naturally. Primal therapy wasn't all about screaming, but the title of his book has left us with images of people having gone away for grim weekends where they'd spend hours rolling around the floor in the foetal position, wailing loudly; these days you could have a weekend at the seaside for a fraction of the cost, half the trauma, and about the same degree of improvement in mental health.

John Lennon and Yoko Ono loved it. But since the 1970s it has been widely criticized as offering no benefit beyond placebo – unless you value slight hoarseness and a hankering for a lozenge. Depressingly for Janov, the most lasting legacy could be said to be the music of Tears For Fears, whose name and a number of lyrics were inspired by his writings. When the band met Janov in the mid-1980s, they were said to be disappointed by how "Hollywood" he was, and they showed little interest in his suggestion that they write a musical.

Getting fit using a massive motorized elastic band

As we become lazier and more spherical, we become increasingly seduced by the of idea shedding excess flab without breaking a sweat. We search high and low for solutions that act upon us, without us having to do anything other than standing still, or preferably sitting or even lying still. Massage belts (or "electro arse-band dewobblifiers", to give them their scientific name) looked like the reassembly of the internal components of a washing machine into a catapult-like harness; by standing in a variety of positions, parts of your body would be vigorously pummelled by the rubber sheet, while anyone watching would picture the lazy chubster being sent pinging majestically through the nearest bay window.

It doesn't take a genius to realize that the cardio-vascular benefits of being shaken about a bit are virtually non-existent, and while there may have been some toning of the muscles, the health improvements were more mental than physical – that is "well, at least I'm doing something." The massage belt now forms the lower strata of decades of home exercise equipment thrown into landfill, while magic pills and power plates continue to tease us with the possibility of losing weight fast. But we're wiser now. Aren't we?

Relieving the monotony of sporting events by streaking

The winter of 1973–74 saw the practice of running around in public places with no clothes on become strangely popular across student campuses in the USA. On 7 March 1974, the record for the largest group streak was set by 1543 assertive, confident young students at the University of Georgia; four weeks later a Mr Robert Opel nudely interrupted David Niven during the Academy Awards ceremony, and the phenomenon began to spread globally.

Michael O'Brien cut a Christ-like figure during his naked sprint at an England rugby international in April 1974; Michael Angelow straddled the stumps during an Ashes Test Match the following summer, and by the time Erica Roe completed her topless streak at another rugby match in 1982, the police helmet had been firmly established as the modern-day fig leaf. The streakers' motivation? Women have tended to do well financially out of their escapades; blokes did it more as an act of drunken defiance. But as more sporting events were interrupted by people desperately seeking fame, TV companies started cutting away and showing uninteresting areas of grass in order to dissuade them, and today streaking is seen more as a worrying symbol of inadequate security than a much-needed livening-up of the on-field action.

Having a portrait of a reigning monarch on your crockery

These days it seems like a strange way to express one's patriotism; to buy mugs or plates that prominently feature the head of the reigning monarch, and then either noisily slurp tea from an area just above their crown, or dump some fish and chips squarely on their face and leave it smeared with the congealing remains of a dollop of tomato ketchup. But as Britain roared its approval during the summer of the Queen's silver jubilee in 1977, it was almost seen as your civic duty to purchase a set of commemorative crockery.

It's interesting to ponder where all these millions of pieces of kitchenware have disappeared to. Unearthing one in your garage or your loft has people peering at them in awe; even a mug commemorating the imminent wedding of Prince Charles and Lady Diana Spencer – with a suitable saccharine portrait – seems like something from another century. Oh, it is. You could put it down to declining patriotism or a disinterest in the monarchy, but millions proudly waved the flag for the Queen's golden jubilee. They just didn't want a mug.

Laughing uproariously at borderline racist sitcoms

History continues to throw up appalling examples of racism, and while whole nations (naming no names) have considered such attitudes to be a great idea at the time, they don't really belong in a slightly frivolous book such as this one. Mild racism masquerading as teatime entertainment, however, is something that has, thankfully, been consigned to the dustbin of history.

Programmes such as *Till Death Us Do Part*, *Love Thy Neighbour* (dealing with the reactions of a white couple to a black couple moving in next door) and *Curry And Chips*, featuring a blacked-up Spike Milligan as a Pakistani factory worker in conflict with his colleagues, weren't written by racists – indeed, the white characters were invariably portrayed as the ignorant and bigoted ones. But the most overtly racist language often got the biggest laughs, and many black or Asian people found that language being hurled back at them on the street. It's almost impossible to watch sections of these programmes today without covering ones eyes and wincing slightly, and that embarrassment we feel is a measure of how attitudes have changed over the last forty years.

Paying to roller-skate for three hours around an ovoid rink

Ice-skating conjures up a picture of a couple gliding effortlessly around a sparkling rink, performing triple toe loops and double salkos while wearing glinting, inscrutable smiles. Roller disco, however, has very different images associated with it: groups of teenagers, clumsily galumphing their way around an ovoid expanse of floor, eyes wide, arms stuck out in front of them (just in case), the clack and thud of the skates all but drowning out the sound of "Yes Sir, I Can Boogie" by Baccara. Elegance isn't the first word that springs to mind.

This wasn't anything to do with dancing. It was more like going for an unsteady walk. Of course, the American sport of roller derby was

basically a test of
endurance as people
roller-skated around a
circuit for hours on end,
but combining it with
popular music created a
social occasion – first for kids
to meet each other, then fall over
each other, and then pick each other up off the
floor, if they were lucky. Roller-disco has been re-emerging of late,
but it shouldn't be long before it's popped back into the time capsule.

Putting one's keys in a bowl at a party for someone other than one's wife to fish out

The free-and-easy partner-swapping that's supposed to have taken place
in middle-class suburbia during the 1970s was only ever something
that happened to other people, in the same way that those university
campuses that were supposedly a hotbed of promiscuity were actually
full of socially inhibited students writing bad poetry.

But key parties helped the trend along, if indeed it occurred at all;
couples put their keys in a bowl, crossed their fingers and hoped fervently
for the best. The women picked out a bunch of keys, and then spent
a short period of time engaging in embarrassed, disappointing sex
with whoever owned the keys in question. The 1997 film *The Ice Storm*,
starring Kevin Kline and Sigourney Weaver, depicted this kind of thing
going on in Connecticut in 1973, and while such parties are commonly
thought of as being risqué, thrilling and oodles of fun, it was probably
exactly like this film – a bitter cauldron of jealousy and recrimination.
You might think monogamy is boring, but at least it doesn't leave you
with a venereal disease, and a nagging, unpleasant memory of the
grimacing face of some bloke you barely know called Jim.

Decorating walls with pictures made out of nails and string

Humans have hung some pretty unpleasant things on their walls over the centuries, from animal heads to neatly framed Victorian cartoons where a greengrocer compliments a well-endowed female customer for having an "enormous pear". The tasteful choice during the 1970s, however, was nail and string art. Get a board. Cover it in felt – black, for the most sophisticated results; hammer nails into it in a geometrically pleasing pattern, and then wind silver thread around the nails to create a matrix of geometric miserablism.

These things didn't look like anything in particular. They weren't meant to. But while it's possible to derive a certain amount of enjoyment from their regularity and neatness, you could say the same about a ball bearing. Spirograph was the parallel for the younger generation; again, you were able to make "art" without any discernable talent other than an ability to follow some instructions. There were more wall-mounted horrors to follow in the 1980s, but it's a relief to know that the austere white wall won the day eventually.

Attempt to create an Etch-A-Sketch masterpiece

Who knows how many promising young artists have had their ambition clobbered out of them by the sheer frustration of being unable to draw anything on the silvery Etch-A-Sketch screen, except perhaps a staircase viewed from side-on, or a primitive television set. Which is precisely what the Etch-A-Sketch looked like. Turn one knob for a horizontal line, the other for vertical, and both together – slowly and exceptionally carefully – to produce a diagonal line. The achievement of drawing a circle was something akin to watchmaking or defusing explosives. The only satisfying aspect of the toy was the ease with which you could erase your miserable efforts and either start again or, more likely, quietly kick the thing under the bed.

It's hard to see why Etch-A-Sketch provokes such fond memories. Thanks to the magic of the Internet we can see people producing incredibly intricate portraits of popstars or heads of state using one – but these people are one-in-a-million superhumans. It was billed as "the ultimate doodling tool" – but despite huge sales, that title is still held firmly by the humble pencil and paper.

Aerobic larks and abandoning Marx: The Eighties

It was known as the "me" decade, the one where "should I, shouldn't I" was finally replaced with "I will! I will! I did! Oh, I wish I hadn't". As countries attempted to haul themselves out of another recession in preparation for the next, the younger generation became obsessed with the brash, the dayglo and the electronic, while their parents did their utmost to remain sensible, sombre and analogue.

We had to cope with hypercolour sweatshirts, left-wing terrorism and AIDS, although fortunately not in the same weekend; we wore Katherine Hamnett T-shirts without realizing they carried anti-abortion slogans, gyrated provocatively to music that emerged from gay discos, and donated our pocket money to famine-stricken Ethiopia after being harangued to do so by a furious-looking Bob Geldof. It was a decade like no other, mainly because that's just how the space-time continuum works.

Wearing deely boppers in an attempt to appear approachable

We find some aspects of the natural world so beautiful that we try to incorporate the look into our homes or our outfits. Snakeskin handbags, fox-fur stoles, floral-print curtains, those cat-paw slippers with claws at the front. Not to everyone's taste, granted – but aesthetically speaking you'd have to admit that these examples are several leagues above making yourself look like some kind of space-age insect with flapping antennae.

1982 was the year of the deely bopper, or the beany bopper, space bopper, bonce bopper or "those headbands with things on". The person who had the idea has wisely decided not to own up to it, but the offending item seems to have emerged in New York and then spread to Britain during that summer via tabloid newspapers who described them as a "hot new American trend". Nearly all of America was, at best, ambivalent about the deely bopper, but the British started buying them anyway. Pre-teenagers could just about get away with the futuristic snail look. But alarm bells sounded when middle-aged receptionists without a shred of dignity started sporting them, explaining that "I'm mad, me. Mad. Ask anyone."

Taking out an endowment policy to pay for your home

The world is still reeling from the foolhardy, self-interested actions of the global banking system. But the vast majority of us are as bewildered by the laws of economics as we are by differential calculus, so we're happy to take advice from anyone in a suit with a briefcase and an approachable manner. When they tell us that they're the best ones to look after our money, we believe them, and never consider for a moment that greed might be their motivation. But as greed is our motivation, it shouldn't be much of a surprise.

The 1980s saw the financial world come up with a fresh new approach to paying off the mortgage on your home: don't pay it off at all. Just pay the interest, and invest some more money in the hope that it'll magically grow to the size of the loan by the time it's due for repayment. We were promised returns of ten, or even twelve percent, and that we could well have a pot of spare cash at the end of it. Unfortunately, returns were more like four percent, and lenders were eventually forced to admit that the whole plan was flawed, and that our investments were falling well short. Mis-sold endowments spawned their own flourishing industry based on clawing back some compensation, while "endowment mortgage" became as dirty a pair of words as "crack whore".

Making yourself appear much heavier by wearing a shell suit

Tracksuits look great on the people who were designed to wear them. Athletes. Not those whose idea of sporting activity involves lolling on a sofa and watching wrestling while consuming deep-fried potato and belching loudly. Tragically, the things that make tracksuits ideal for athletes – easy to get on and off, lightweight, comfortable – also appeal to those of a more spherical build, and nothing kills off a fashion faster than its rapid adoption by people who look terrible while wearing it.

But shellsuits took the tracksuit somewhere even more dark and sinister. We're not just talking garish colour schemes here (and they certainly were garish, with bright green and purple being one inexplicably popular choice) – they simply made chubby people look obese, and obese people look like barrage balloons. By elasticating all the areas where the body emerged – wrists, ankles, waist, neck – and constructing the garment out of a parachute-like material, the contours of the body were replaced with a new set of even more unflattering contours. Add to this the fact that it felt as tactile as a shower cap, and that you could clearly hear people's thighs scraping together as they approached, and it adds up to a piece of clothing as diametrically opposed to the sensuous glamour of the velvet smoking jacket as it's possible to get.

Communicating to lonely lorry drivers via CB radio

The Internet has made us blasé about communicating with strangers. In fact, after one too many slanging matches on online forums, the whole concept can start to lose its appeal. But 1970s films such as *Smokey And The Bandit* and *Convoy* led to a surge in interest in Citizens Band Radio, and governments in both the US and the UK were forced to relax laws to allow us to mumble incomprehensible jargon into plastic handsets and hope for a crackling reply from someone we didn't know.

In the US, a license was originally needed to use CB, but repeated flouting of the law led to this requirement being dropped. In the UK, it was illegal to use one at all, but again, the sheer number of people using imported radios forced the government's hand. Christmas 1981 saw CB become one of the top UK gift ideas – and in turn saw it become the victim of its own popularity. Channels were swamped with people trying and failing to master the intricacies of the NATO phonetic alphabet, repeatedly asking "good buddies" for an "eyeball", or just swearing loudly and repeatedly. CBs were henceforth quietly packed away and left under the stairs – a perfect example of the idea being way more exciting than the reality. The ubiquity of mobile phones has made CB look like a particularly unusual relic.

Becoming obsessed with a three-dimensional hand-held puzzle

The 3x3x3 multicoloured cube invented by Ernö Rubik is generally considered to be the world's best-selling toy. Bearing in mind that it generated frustration rather than excitement, could only be used by one person at a time, and was unsolvable by normal human beings unless they'd referred to books entitled something like "How to solve the Rubik's Cube", this is a pretty astonishing achievement. And the fact that most of its sales were concentrated in the first half of the 1980s indicates how enormously successful it was during that period.

While those of us who felt oppressed by the cube removed and reattached its stickers or hacked it to pieces with a screwdriver in order to achieve some kind of pyrrhic victory over it, those who studied and memorized the optimum methods of cube solving would engage each other in speed trials. Their cubes were greased with Vaseline and primed for action – but by that stage it had stopped being a puzzle, and started being about following instructions very quickly. People even started solving it underwater in a single breath; fortunately their impulse to stay alive proved greater than their need to solve the cube, and as far as we know, no one died.

Collecting stationery that smelled nice

Erasers perform one very simple function: removing pencil marks from paper. As activities go, it's pretty mundane – at least it was until enterprising stationery companies decided to liven up erasing with a range of exciting aromas. You might think there'd be as much point in this as manufacturing a smelly door or a tasty car, but kids loved it – and collecting delicately perfumed erasers became a popular and relatively inexpensive hobby.

But in the UK this was suddenly curtailed by the British government with the introduction of its "Scented Erasers Safety Order 1984". No joke. There was widespread concern that small children – who, after all, enjoy putting unusual objects in their mouths – would turn erasers into a potential choking hazard. Most children would have discovered that they taste far less pleasant than they smell and rapidly spat them out – but the order came into effect regardless. One panicking importer who found himself stuck with £270,000 worth of unsellable stock decided to challenge the ruling, pointing out that children are far more likely to choke on a piece of fruit; the government conceded that this may be true, but people need to eat fruit, and don't really need to rub out pencil marks with something that smells nice. These days, no sensory pleasure can be derived from correcting drawing errors. None.

Wearing leg warmers because the girls on *Fame* did

The term "leg warmer" is a bit misleading. A more correct description might be "shin concealer"; that does make them sound utterly pointless but, frankly, they were. True, dancers could conceivably give their calf muscles an extra layer of protection from the vicious elements that one experiences in the average gym or dance studio, but they were happy to leave their feet and thighs exposed to those wild oscillations in temperature, and the lower leg isn't generally regarded as a dangerous area for heat loss. Ask any polar explorer.

OK, so we've established that they probably served little purpose. So why were they so popular? Could it have been merely to expand the circumference of the shin? Part of the blame can be laid at the door of the films *Fame* and *Flashdance*, which featured hundreds of aspiring stars of the future wearing leotards, ballet pumps and leg warmers. But how they reached the silver screen in the first place is a mystery. Perhaps it's the fault of the person who came up with the toilet roll cover (see p.132).

Considering "liver in lager" to be an exciting food innovation

The world of high-class French cuisine experienced something of a revolution in the 1970s, as the rich sauces of haute cuisine were replaced by the "nouvelle cuisine" of chefs such as Paul Bocuse: speedy cooking processes, fresh ingredients, inventive and attractive dishes. French citizens who could afford to eat in top restaurants understood these innovations, because they recognized the tradition that they were rejecting.

But when the idea finally reached places like Britain, nouvelle cuisine was suddenly synonymous with food that a) came in exceedingly small portions, and b) contained horribly incompatible ingredients. Ambitious chefs, eager to be seen as cutting edge, would place two small mounds of contrasting food on a colossal white plate, draw some kind of hieroglyph on the side using an unctuous *jus*, and charge £20 for it. "Where's the food?" asked bemused diners, who weren't used to having to buy three Mars Bars on the way home to fill themselves up after a meal out. Nouvelle cuisine became heavily satirized (Mike Leigh's *Life Is Sweet* featured king prawn in jam sauce, saveloy on a bed of lychees, and lamb tongues in a rhubarb hollandaise) – but its innovations eventually became more sensibly incorporated into modern dining, and we were eventually allowed to say farewell to meals that resembled overpriced minimalist paintings.

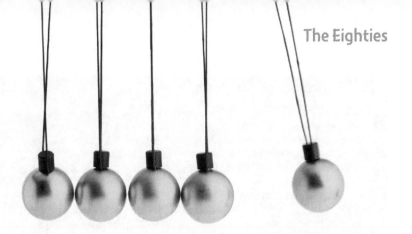

Distracting yourself from work with an executive toy

There's barely anything more offensive to the average hard-working citizen than the notion of highly paid executives having so much time on their hands that they spend precious hours mucking about with objects on their desk. If bus drivers or nurses casually interrupted their own working day to idly explore the concept of perpetual motion using a bit of swinging chrome, they'd be told to get back to work, or be sacked. Executives, however, just received a polite enquiry as to whether they were having a nice day at the office. Which they probably were, and especially on that kind of salary.

Newton's cradle is perhaps the best known of these toys; popular in the 1970s, it featured five spheroids suspended from a metal frame, rocking to and fro to neatly prove the law of conservation of linear momentum. By the 1980s, however, we had Japanese zen rock gardens, sunburst fibre optics, and pin art. Pin art, in all its chrome and black glory, consisted of a vertical surface into which were embedded closely packed horizontal pins. If you pushed an object into one side, a representation of it – in pins – would emerge from the other. And you could happily repeat this until the conference call finally came through from LA. These days the Internet has successfully replaced the executive toy by cleverly allowing you to waste time while appearing to be working.

Put that in your pipe and smoke it: sayings that have lost their currency

It's a crying shame that audio recordings were only invented in 1877. How disappointing that we'll never get to hear the measured tones of, say, Oliver Cromwell, and discover to our surprise that he had his own catchphrase which he'd deploy in moments of stress, something like "The shops are now open, madam." The patterns of speech in medieval times might have been utterly thrilling to the modern ear – and, even more excitingly, they might have thrown in phrases and colloquialisms that would have us furrowing our brows in disbelief. In the same way that they'd be nonplussed by seeing crowds of teenage boys repeatedly yelling "Wasssuuup" at each other. And even more nonplussed when we attempted to explain Budweiser to them. Or commercials. Or television.

We also find "Wasssuuup" pretty irritating these days; popular sayings simply fall out of favour – either because their reference points have disappeared, or we've found a new way of expressing the same idea, or because sheer repetition has utterly devalued it. In the 1980s, British men would imitate comedian Harry Enfield by waving a wad of notes at their chortling friends, and shouting "Loadsamoney!" Today, this would be met with disbelief bordering on contempt. In the same way, Americans tend not to say "where's the beef?" when they feel short-changed, because they'd sound as if they'd just awoken from 25 years in a coma.

But some phrases, long since abandoned, could do with being rehabilitated. Imagine the joy you'd feel if you leapt into a taxi and shrieked at the driver: "Home, James, and don't spare the horses!" If we had the slightest recollection of the Battle of Warburg in 1760, and the fact that the Marquis of Granby lost his hat during a cavalry charge, we might still say "going bald-headed for something" to indicate bravery. Few of us have a copy of Edward Cocker's wildly popular and influential 1677 Maths textbook *Arithmetick* on our shelves, but if we did, we'd still describe anything that was absolutely correct as "according to Cocker". We don't describe honoured guests as being "above the salt", or a woman's scolding of her husband as a "curtain lecture". If someone makes a preposterous suggestion we don't say "the answer's a lemon", and we don't announce the purchase of a round of drinks by saying "bumpers all round and no heel taps", more's the pity.

But we've been happy to see the back of more recent popular phrases and sayings. For years, British children would call each other "Joey", in a reference to a disabled man by the name of Joey Deacon who appeared occasionally on kids' TV show *Blue Peter* – and adults of a certain age will still lapse into it when they've had too much to drink. We've been trying to get rid of "Put that in your pipe and smoke it" for a good 150 years, but still people come out with it when they're feeling slightly smug. British comedy shows gave us "hello sailor", "that's your mum that is," "steps back in amazement" and "ooh, I could crush a grape" – all of which are infused with the atmosphere of the period in which they originated. Affixing "not" to the end of our sentences to indicate sarcasm feels inappropriate in a post-*Wayne's World*-world, as does screeching "Aciiiiiieeeeed" while dancing at clubs – but these were both things that we were delighted to do a few years ago.

You can't force the pace of change ("bad" might mean "good", "wicked" might mean "even better", "bloody awful" will always mean "terrible") but you can bet that describing something as "well nang" will feel dated by the time this book is published. If it isn't already.

the shops are now open, madam

Hanging mass-produced art on the walls of your home

Not many of us have the millions of pounds required to put an original work by a respected master in our kitchen. In the absence of a Vermeer or a Magritte, we might turn instead to an artistic friend and commission him or her to come up with something "not too tasteless" to fill up the empty space. Or perhaps put up some daubs done at school by our kids, in order to make absolutely certain that they feel some kind of embarrassment as they get older.

But the 1980s saw poster company Athena shift millions of copies of one particular poster called *Man and Baby*, featuring a rugged hunk showing affection towards a gurgling infant, and it became a sophisticated decoration choice for the thinking woman. It symbolized the "New Man" that they were probably keen to meet – a man who wouldn't come home hours after the baby had been put to bed, and drunkenly bellow for his dinner before demanding sex. The model, Adam Perry, demonstrated zero New Man credentials by sleeping with three thousand women as a result of his appearance on the poster; he intended to write a book about his experiences, but conceded that it "got a bit boring". The original posters have long since been rolled up and shoved in the attic, and if you see one today it'll only have been put there in a knowing, ironic way. Not the fate, you'll notice, of a Vermeer or a Magritte.

Maintaining a weird collection of Cabbage Patch dolls

They looked odd, they didn't perform any useful function, and yet grown adults would traverse continents in order to get their hands on one. This was ostensibly for their children, but the sheer desperation with which Cabbage Patch dolls would be pursued – including pitched battles in toy stores – gives a clear indication that the craze was driven as much by parents as by kids.

They were invented in 1978 by Debbie Morehead and Xavier Roberts. You might think it a bit rich to use words like "invented" when referring to a doll that contained no electrical circuits, didn't wet itself or say "ma ma" in a robotic monotone. But their stroke of genius was to create a mass-produced toy where every one differed slightly in appearance, and came with its own adoption certificate from the Babyland General Hospital. For some reason the idea of taking guardianship over a helpless young orphan – albeit one that was made of cloth and incapable of sentient thought – proved to be remarkably appealing. Whether the desperate pursuit of the toy was fuelled by the company simply failing to keep up with demand is unclear – but, rather like the Pet Rock (see p.142) the Cabbage Patch doll ended up having a disproportionate emotional hold over its owners, and indeed those who scoured stores in the hope of finding one.

Exercising while watching a woman in a leotard on breakfast television

It's hard to imagine, now that we're in an age of 24-hour rolling news and can play roulette on our TVs at 5am if we want to, that the idea of turning on the television at breakfast time on weekdays in 1980s Britain was almost viewed as immoral. TV was an entertainment source intended for evening consumption with the family, or for lifting depressed housewives out of mid-afternoon boredom. So when breakfast television was introduced in the UK in 1983, it was regarded with suspicion – rather like someone who turns up on your doorstep claiming to be your long-lost cousin, and then starts asking lots of questions about your finances.

The best remembered stars of breakfast TV were aerobics instructors. No doubt prompted by the colossal success of the launch of Jane Fonda's workout videos the previous year, women in leotards were employed to get us working up a sweat in our front rooms. The fact that 99 percent of viewers watched them from a comfortable armchair while shovelling sugar-frosted cereals into their faces didn't seem to matter; we were delighted by their untrammelled enthusiasm for stretching, kicking and lunging. By the 1990s, the sheer futility of attempting to get the public fit saw the practice largely abandoned, and we watched people deliver celebrity gossip or bake cakes instead, while continuing to eat sugar-frosted cereals from the comfort of the same armchair.

Thinking that the state probably knew best

For 45 years following World War II, the West repeatedly restated its distaste for communism. Indeed, you could say that we were only driven through the 50s, 60s and 70s by our need to combat the communist threat. However, during this period, individual governments were combating economic problems by nationalizing industries, hiking up top rates of tax and implementing levels of state control that seem extraordinary by today's standards. But the election of Margaret Thatcher in the UK in 1979, and Ronald Reagan in the US the following year, saw neo-liberals pledge their undying faith in market forces and "rolling back the frontiers of the state". High taxation and regulatory control of the business world were suddenly deemed horribly damaging to private enterprise, and by the middle of the decade it was unlikely that any Western politician would be elected to high office unless they were a staunch believer in the capitalist dream. Socialist parties desperately attempted to shrug off far-left influences in order to become acceptable to the electorate.

In Eastern Europe, of course, there was no electorate, because there were no meaningful elections; the level of state control extended to not giving people the opportunity to disagree – a situation that slowly grew from mild frustration to full-blooded revolution. By the end of the 1980s, decades of Marxist thought were finally abandoned as a bad job. As to whether this was the right decision, we'll have to wait and see…

Rolling up the sleeves of your jacket in order to appear both sexy and interesting

The dovetailing of smart and casual can be slightly awkward – think jeans and brogues, or dinner suits with trainers – but for some reason the stylings of *Miami Vice*'s Crockett and Tubbs became, as one writer put it, "the biggest fashion influence since the Nehru jacket". Pastel suits were worn with T-shirts, shoes were worn without socks – not a look that would get you a dinner table in a posh hotel, but millions of men chose to emulate the crime-fighting duo by equipping themselves with an untailored, baggy faux-Armani linen suit and rolling up the sleeves.

It's not clear why the exposure of ones forearms should have provoked such admiration in women (one fan of the retro look tells of how it "made men look so strong, sexy and interesting".) Perhaps it was just the combination of the smartness of a suit with the workmanlike sleeve-push, as if you were preparing to "get the job done". (In the case of *Miami Vice*, of course, this was generally the arrest and imprisonment of drug barons.) When men started attempting it using tailored suits, thus making themselves look as if they'd put on a smaller man's clothes by mistake, the fad was already over. Thankfully, it was not succeeded by the cummerbund plus Hawaiian shorts combo.

Expressing fury at being ordered to wear a seat belt

"You won't catch me wearing some kind of baby harness", you'd hear proud men boasting throughout the 1970s, as public information films and newspaper articles described the ways in which wearing a seat belt might prevent you from being projected through your car windscreen at high velocity. Certainly in the UK and USA, men could happily brush aside this advice, because advice is all that it was. But following the lead of other Western nations, it became a legal requirement to wear a seat belt in the front seats of a car – first in the UK in 1983, and then in the US, on a state-by-state basis, the following year.

The average man is incredibly defensive about his ability to operate a motor vehicle. He might speed down the motorway while burrowing in the glove compartment for a travel sweet while telling terrified passengers to stop complaining because he's never had an accident. So the fact that the authorities were handing out unwanted advice on how not to maim and kill their passengers didn't go down well. People would loudly protest about civil liberties; even videos showing eggs being smashed when rattling around in boxes did little to convince them. The occasional diehard still spends time unearthing data to try to prove how ineffective seat-belt wearing is, or that it's somehow dangerous to other road users – but now we're generally happy to clunk, click and accept it.

Collecting ring pulls from cans in the hope that it would change someone's life

No one knows quite how the rumour started, or quite how the misconception took hold. But the 1980s saw the spirited collection of ring pulls, or pull tabs, from drink cans in the hope that it would somehow benefit the needy. Those suffering from kidney failure were thought to particularly benefit from the hoarding of small pieces of aluminium alloy; benevolent groups would mobilize, glug their way through thousands upon thousands of gallons of soft drinks, carefully pop the ring pull in a bag, and chuck the can away.

But the ring pull was no more valuable than the can itself. Almost worthless, in fact. Charity groups and the aluminium industry tried their best to get the word out that there was little point in collecting them, but to no avail; people got terribly upset that their million ring pulls were worth a couple of hundred dollars at best, when they'd been told it would pay for a dialysis machine. Thanks to the Internet, similar rumours have resurged of late – that a thousand of the new-style tabs (much harder to pull off, incidentally) will pay for one chemotherapy treatment session. Sadly, this is untrue. It doesn't even cover the dental bills of the people who've put away an astonishing quantity of sugary drinks.

Reading books that had several different potential endings

Sometimes stories don't always turn out the way you want. You're primed for a happy ending, but the heroine suddenly gets a gangrenous foot and has to have it amputated. A detective's inability to piece together the most obvious of clues leaves a serial killer free to continue his murderous rampage through Luxembourg. But the 1980s saw a genre of books published that allowed you to affect the outcome of the story by making the big plot decisions yourself, and then turning to the relevant page to see what happened. (They were all written, somewhat disconcertingly, in the second person, so it wasn't the character of Omok who vanquished the evil overlords of Thaak – it was you.)

The *Choose Your Own Adventure* and *Fighting Fantasy* series were both incredibly popular, although bringing chance and probability into a book format inevitably led to people cheating in order to get the outcome they wanted. If you turned to page 96 and discovered that you were about to be maimed by a dragon, you'd just turn back to page 50 and choose to go down the path to the magic forest on page 92 instead. By the time you were halfway through the book, the corners of the pages had been decimated for convenient bookmarking purposes. The format was much more suited to video games that didn't give you so much of an opportunity to cheat – and as soon as microprocessors could cope, that's exactly what happened.

Extending the width of your torso several inches by wearing shoulder pads

These days we're enlightened enough to understand that women can demonstrate superiority over men in the workplace by simply coming up with better ideas and being more efficient than them. But in the 1980s, there was a feeling that they had to compete physically by "power dressing". They were probably right; chauvinists would have sneered if women had dared to compete while wearing something understated and feminine, so trouser suits were donned, and broad-shouldered jackets were fearsomely padded at the shoulders with foam. (The idea of wearing false beards and pointlessly tinkering with cars was postponed in case more drastic action ever needed to be taken.)

While the fashion was slimming – tapering as it did from colossal shoulders to the waist – it also reshaped the female form into a peculiar equilateral triangle. But such was the influence of programmes like *Dynasty* and *Dallas*, where female characters could only get through doors by turning sideways, that shoulder pads were adopted wholesale by high-street fashion chains. Fortunately, the need to dress powerfully ebbed away towards the end of the decade, and at some point in the 1990s shoulder pads disappeared – or, at least, shrunk to a more anatomically sympathetic size.

Applying overwhelming perfumes to your wrists and neck

There are always people who go too far in attempting to impress by allowing their own personal odor to be utterly obliterated by over-generous application of bottled perfume or deodorant. We know from bitter experience that the more you apply doesn't necessarily make for a more positive outcome – indeed, noses wrinkle, windows are opened, and in extreme cases you'll be escorted from the premises.

1980s perfumes such as Christian Dior's Poison and, pre-eminently, Giorgio Beverly Hills, were notable for their brute strength, regardless of how sparingly you tried to apply them. Passers-by would be overwhelmed with salvoes of bergamot or vanilla – not so much notes, as fully-fledged symphonies. Giorgio is still described by the manufacturer as conveying "glamour, sophistication and the promise of adventure", but the only adventure you'd have in New York City in the 1980s would be wandering around town looking for a restaurant that would seat you, the fragrance having been deemed so potent that it ruined the diner's palate. It matched perfectly with the brashness, excess and conspicuous consumption of the day, but we've learned since that resisting the urge to give a potential mate an olefactory clubbing can be somewhat more seductive.

Sugary booze and Celtic tattoos: The Nineties

9

We celebrated the dawn of the final decade of the twentieth century by plunging headlong into another recession, and then desperately looking for ways of getting out of it, or at least taking our minds off it a bit. Computers began to provide a distraction; despite their growing popularity during the 1980s they were still the preserve of the geek squad, but the 1990s saw the birth of the World Wide Web and the realization that it might be of some recreational

use – and subsequently some commercial use. At which point we all rushed to get online, while self-styled entrepreneurs came up with thousands of half-baked ideas for cyber-business ventures that were almost certainly doomed to failure.

The first sheep was cloned and belly buttons were pierced in their millions, while Western Europe came together in union and Yugoslavia unhappily splintered into pieces. We were amused by *The Simpsons*, delighted by the release of Nelson Mandela, nervous about the first Gulf War and morose over the death of Princess Diana – but not so distracted that we couldn't indulge in some mystifying behaviour that looks unusual in hindsight…

Heading into the countryside to take drugs and jump up and down

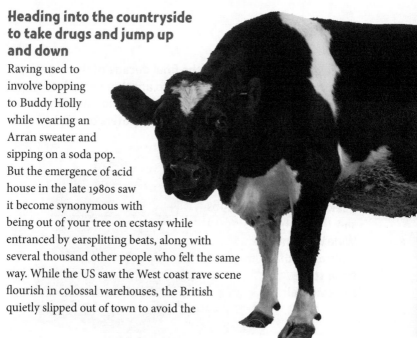

Raving used to involve bopping to Buddy Holly while wearing an Arran sweater and sipping on a soda pop. But the emergence of acid house in the late 1980s saw it become synonymous with being out of your tree on ecstasy while entranced by earsplitting beats, along with several thousand other people who felt the same way. While the US saw the West coast rave scene flourish in colossal warehouses, the British quietly slipped out of town to avoid the inevitable interest from the police. An evening's entertainment would consist of hanging around a phone box waiting for a call from a shifty bloke telling you to head for a particular field in Essex; then you'd drive for hours through winding lanes to find it, only to find that the police knew about it all along. A fantastically British way of enjoying oneself.

But if the police didn't turn up, fun was had in abundance and, predictably, the authorities got the fear. Laws were brought in to enable police to stop large groups of people listening to (as the law put it): "sounds wholly or predominantly characterized by the emission of a succession of repetitive beats." This effectively killed off a movement that wasn't keen on being properly licensed, so everyone went home and waited for the next opportunity to spontaneously gather overnight in huge crowds and take large quantities of drugs. They're still waiting.

Nurturing an electronic pet

Humans can direct their caring instincts towards the unlikeliest of things. Tortoises don't show any reciprocal love and self-centredly hoover up displays of affection (that is, provision of lettuce leaves and a cardboard box.) Pet rocks (see p.142) are even less appreciative, retaining the same rock-like demeanour whether we bother to look after them or not. The Japanese Tamagotchi, however, which became hugely popular in the mid to late 1990s, was simultaneously undeserving of affection (it was plastic) but also incredibly demanding. Designed to emit loud beeping noises when distressed, it had children rushing to its aid to either feed it, clean it or play with it, via the complex emotional interaction afforded by pressing buttons A, B or C.

Earlier models could potentially starve to "death" in a few hours if you were too busy worrying about real-life issues, so the toys began accompanying children to school, where lessons would be interrupted for urgent feeding sessions. Bandai, the manufacturer, was forced to introduce a "pause" button to allow the Tamagotchi's life to be put on temporary hiatus – and that's when it lost any ability to teach children about life and death. Because real pets can't be paused, and nor do they have reset buttons that let you bring them back to life should you neglect them. Tamagotchi are still around, but most electronic "caring" has now shifted to websites like neopets.com, which are similarly addictive, but at least you don't have to pay for them. And they don't beep at you from under the bed.

Playing amateur football wearing a nose-bandage in order to improve your performance

It's not the taking part that counts in sport, it's the winning – and athletes will go to great lengths to gain that competitive advantage over their opponents. While replacing your limbs with bionic, fuel-injected cylinders or injecting beta-blockers into your groin is not condoned by sport's ruling bodies, no one could reasonably object to anyone wearing a sticking plaster over the bridge of the nose. Sportsmen, particularly footballers, started doing just that, and thousands of amateurs copied the look, running around local parks as if they were auditioning for a low-budget stage production about the life of Adam Ant. But what did it actually do?

Not a great deal. The theory behind it is sound enough: it slightly widens the nasal passages, allowing you to breathe through your nose more easily – which is why mouth-breathing snorers don't disturb their partners quite as much when they wear these strips, as it helps them to keep their mouths shut. But if you need more air when you're running around, well, you open your mouth. So nasal strips offer no benefit to footballers, squash players or cyclists, unless they discover that their jaws are wired shut and their lips superglued together. (Rare.) By 2000, the fad disappeared as people realized that it attracted hoots of derision rather than medals and trophies.

Excitedly swapping small cardboard discs

It's the dream of any toy manufacturer to hit upon an idea that becomes hugely collectible, but is also dirt cheap to produce. Normally we're wise to the inherent worthlessness of everyday objects, which is why plastic cups don't change hands for hundreds of dollars on eBay, and there aren't queues down the high street for soil. But occasionally our guard inexplicably drops – and one of those moments was when Pogs suddenly made whole nations of children go nuts for small circles of cardboard.

Pogging originated in Hawaii in the 1920s, when the cardboard caps on bottles of milk were used by those in the dairy delivery business to fill idle moments with a quick game. Stack a number of the pogs face-down into a tower; take another pog and throw it at the stack, with the aim of upturning as many pogs as possible. The ones you flipped over, you kept. Repeat until bored. When a Hawaiian teacher reintroduced the game to a maths class in 1991 (presumably to teach them how to count upturned circles of cardboard) a craze began, and was made more frenzied by the collecting and trading of pogs emblazoned with the faces

of Aerosmith, or Power Rangers, or Michael Jordan. But the allure couldn't last, and today huge collections sit in tubes in cupboards while kids blast their enemies to pieces in *World Of Warcraft* instead.

Creating new exciting cuisines by fusing Eastern and Western flavours

National cuisines are the product of slow evolution, a complex interweaving of ingredients and flavours based on centuries of trial and error. Fusion cuisine of the 1990s was often based on scant minutes of trial and error. And mainly error. There's nothing wrong with innovation in the kitchen, of course – otherwise we'd all be subsisting on hunks of bison meat torn from the carcass with our bare hands – but fusion cuisine would create a head-on collision between, say, Thai and Spanish cookery, for no other reason than raising a few eyebrows.

It's telling that the proponents of misguided fusion cooking largely kept their activities well away from the countries whose culinary traditions they were despoiling; while the British might happily wander into a Chino-Argentinian restaurant in search of sustenance, such an establishment in Beijing or Buenos Aires would have caused untold consternation and distress. If we learned one thing from 1990s fusion, it's that you can't stick soy sauce and ginger on a plate of non-Eastern food, call it exotic, price it at $20 and hope to get away with it. These days, practically every chef drones on about how they "use the best ingredients and treat them simply"; this refrain may be annoying, but it's nowhere near as annoying as, say, sushi stroganoff.

Refusing to pay your taxes

No government really expects the electorate to enthusiastically embrace the idea of paying more tax, which is why they're invariably introduced via the back door and concealed as "exciting new initiatives". But most of us – aside from large corporations, who just shift all their assets offshore – usually just grumble a bit on the Internet and pay up because we're not that keen on being arrested. But there are situations where we're pushed to the point of civil disobedience. The introduction of a poll tax for every English citizen was incredibly unpopular in the fourteenth century, and eventually prompted the Peasants' Revolt. But when a similar tax – rebranded the "community charge" to make it seem more cuddly – was introduced in England and Wales in 1990, the authorities, imagining us to be a supine bunch, probably didn't imagine that tens of thousands of people would descend on London to protest. But they did.

And even more striking, people who had never broken the law in their lives took a stand and refused to pay it. As the government's records of who lived where were incredibly disorganized and inaccurate, those who were renting flats or houses simply kept moving and became impossible to pursue, while homeowners, knowing that huge swathes of the population were standing shoulder to shoulder with them, refused to cough up. In some areas, thirty percent of the population wasn't paying, and courts were having to deal with thousands upon thousands of cases. Eventually, the anger paid off; in 1993 the less punitive system of council tax was introduced, and we went back to grudgingly paying it.

Jumping from a great height with elastic bands tied to your ankles

There are some things that were clearly never meant to be attempted by human beings. Making Baked Alaska. Getting your tongue pierced. Wearing top hats. twenty-four-hour telethons. But of all the activities that we have inexplicably thrown ourselves into en masse in the hope of experiencing pleasure, bungee jumping has to rank as one of the most insane. David Attenborough returned from the island nation of Vanuatu in the 1950s with footage of local men hurling themselves from great heights with vines tied around their ankles in the hope of proving their masculinity, but it took 25 years for the Western world to begin to think of the act as a leisure pursuit.

Intrepid practitioners of dangerous sports were the first to (literally) take the plunge, but by 1988 the idea of leaping into the blue yonder with only elasticated rope to keep us from smacking into the ground was considered as safe as going on a rollercoaster, and the first commercial bungee jumping ventures started to flourish. Strict safety rules were employed (not least that the length of bungee cord had to be shorter than the distance from the ground) and the vast majority of jumps passed off without incident, but free falling and bouncing around suspended by your ankles was quietly advised against by some doctors, concerned about the effect on your spine, or neck, or blood pressure. When James Bond kicked off the film *Goldeneye* by bungee jumping over a dam in 1995, the activity was already in decline as millions opted for having a nice sit down instead.

Creating a thriving sub-economy based on the resale of Beanie Babies

After we'd managed to wean ourselves off ridiculous numbers of Cabbage Patch dolls (see p.162) it seems almost inconceivable that a few years later we'd be manically grabbing a new soft toy off the shelves. Beanie Babies didn't do a great deal more or less than the Cabbage Patch dolls – they obeyed the laws of gravity, they stayed roughly in the

Contraceptives that either didn't appeal to us, or just didn't work

It's probably no coincidence that the act of procreating, and thereby ensuring the survival of the human species, is a uniquely pleasurable one. But its tragedy is to be so pleasurable that we've had to spend centuries looking for an effective way of experiencing the pleasure without having to deal with the consequent child-rearing. Such has been our desperation that we've resorted to unusual measures – chemical, mechanical and even magical – a few of which did indeed lessen the chance of conceiving, but were mostly as useful as keeping your fingers crossed and hoping for the best.

Many contraceptives of yore look bizarre today because they were based on a fundamental misunderstanding about the mechanics of conception. Not until the late 1600s was it realized that semen was merely a carrier for the sperm, and the discovery that only one of those sperm needed to be successful wasn't made until the late 1800s. Had the magnitude of the task of producing an effective contraceptive been apparent in Roman times, it's unlikely that they'd have bothered continuing with their miserable attempts to use crocodile dung as some kind of barrier, not to mention Pliny the Elder's idea of getting a man to urinate into a jar, and then drowning a lizard in said urine – a process strangely disassociated with the act of sex itself. Subsequent Byzantine medics didn't have much of a clue, either; Aëtius of Amida suggested that a woman ought to carry the tooth of a child as an amulet around her anus. "Which child?" "Doesn't really matter, love, because it doesn't actually work."

Incredibly, with all this ignorance and superstition clouding the issue, some inventions were accidentally moving in the right direction. Viscous substances such as honey marginally slow down the progress of sperm, and acidic ones act as a mild spermicide; so the complex Ancient Egyptian concoction that contained acacia tips (which release lactic acid) could have done the job it was intended to do, although the time consuming process of preparing it would have been a guaranteed passion killer. You may snort, balk or even screech at the idea of using lemon halves as a uterine barrier or pig intestines as condoms, but they both stood more chance of success than attaching severed weasel testicles to your leg, or digging down into a grave and holding the hand of a dead man, both of which were attempted by medieval women who presumably went on to have dozens of children each.

Some methods somehow persisted for hundreds of years despite having no effect whatsoever; drinking the water that a blacksmith had used for cooling metals was attempted by many desperate women, as was the pointless act of vigorously jumping up and down after sex – as if she wasn't tired enough already. And then there was douching. The efficacy of douching was still defended as recently as the twentieth century, with Coca-Cola supposedly having particularly magical powers – although for all the good it did they may as well have mixed it with vodka and enjoyed a post-coital booze-up.

Thankfully, modern medicine has given us a number of effective contraceptives, although some of them have been cumbersome and unpopular (the introduction of the femidom in the 1990s being a good example), while the Pill had the disappointing side-effect of failing to prevent the spread of sexually transmitted infections. Ironically, the most effective method is also the one sanctioned by puritanical religious leaders: abstinence. Unfortunately, it's also the most unrealistic.

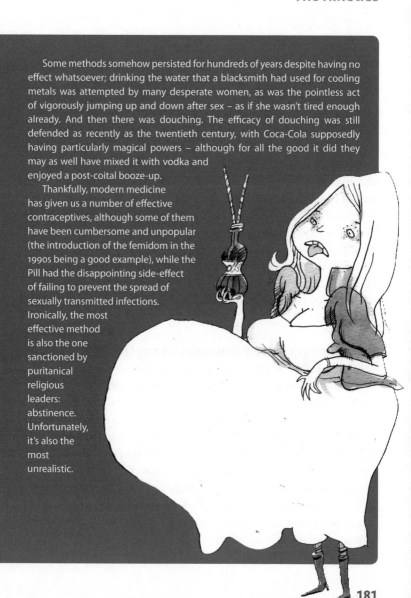

position you'd left them in, and never spontaneously combusted; they were, essentially, just bean bags with faces. But the creator of Beanie Babies, Ty Warner, had undoubtedly taken note of the factors that made Cabbage Patch dolls such a success: give them individual names and a birth date, make them thoroughly collectable, and above all make them a challenge to get hold of.

You couldn't buy them in bigger stores; demand was satisfied via speciality stores and gift shops, but also via classified ads, trade shows, and, most notably, the Internet. For a period in the late 1990s, 822 various types of Beanie Babies were being auctioned on eBay in frenetic festivals of clicking with thousands upon thousands of pounds changing hands. For many people, it was their first auction experience, so the thrill of outbidding someone only added to the rush of getting one's hands on, say, the dark blue version of "Peanut" the elephant. Today, thousands of vintage Beanie Babies, still in mint condition with their various tags intact, barely fetch two dollars. It makes you wonder what it was all for.

Rollerblading rapidly through city centres

The feeling of the wind blowing through your hair is a fairly irresistible one, but the steps you take to experience that minor thrill really need to be offset against any associated inconvenience to others. Rollerblading, or inline skating, had a massive surge of popularity in the mid-1990s, to the point where two-thirds of eleven-year-olds in the USA owned a pair by 1997. And as a result, pavements were blighted with two-speed traffic: pedestrians making their way to and fro at walking speed; and rollerbladers on a series of unspecified urgent missions that required them to dodge anyone who didn't have wheels bolted to the underside of their feet, but frequently left shopping bags upended regardless. Cyclists you can tell to get on the bloody road; not so with rollerbladers.

They were described in the press as the "bane of modern urban society", and the rollerblading masses were certainly easy to despise; with their kneepads, CD Walkmen and blatant disregard for their fellow human beings, they also seemed to be under the impression that they were engaged in a fantastically sexy new sport with the unlikely name of "aggressive skating". This is despite the fact that a set of wheels was doing all the work, and the skaters were burning off fewer calories than those of us who chose to walk. It looked as if the only way of impeding their activities was a return to cobbled streets; but fortunately – whether through new-found consideration for their fellow man or just frustration that we were stopping them going as fast as they would like – they stopped of their own accord.

Wearing copious amounts of body glitter

We don't like to align ourselves with animals of limited intelligence
such as magpies, who are so distracted by shiny objects that they're
incapable of doing anything other than looking at them. But there
is something pleasing about watching something sparkle in an
iridescent fashion, which is probably why there have been a couple
of periods when women chose to adorn themselves with glitter. The
1970s movements of glam rock and disco offered one opportunity, but
things got a little out of hand in the mid to late 1990s, when girls weren't
properly dressed unless their hair, lips, eyes, face, shoulders, décolletage
and legs were slathered in minute metallic crystals. *New York Magazine*
referred to it as a "sparkle epidemic", and roll-on glitter applicators
facilitated mass glitterizing on a hitherto unimaginable scale.

There were two drawbacks for the glitterati. Firstly, that the stuff
got everywhere. There was no process sufficiently thorough to eradicate
all traces of it from your person, it became a permanent feature of the
living-room carpet, bathroom sink and pillowcases, and you'd inevitably
transfer your glitteriness to anyone you came into contact with – which
led to the second problem. Glitter on a man's face became the new
lipstick on the collar – but way, way more difficult to get rid of. Men
would effectively be branded, the glitter would betray them, and there
were no excuses convincing enough to allow them to get away with it.
A few thousand broken relationships and furious hoovering sessions
later, and the glitter fad was no more.

Worrying about the millennium bug

You only need to try getting information out of your bank when their
"system is down" to realize that our lives hang precipitously on the
reliable behaviour of computers. The realization towards the end of the
1980s and throughout the 1990s that many computer programs had been
written, with dubious foresight, to store years with two digits rather than

four – and would thus have trouble coping at midnight on the 1st January 2000 – ended up escalating into a wave of fear mongering that wasn't that far removed from predictions of nuclear war (see p.112). Prime-time television-show hosts urged us to stockpile ten weeks' worth of food, a prominent US politician described the imminent catastrophe as an "electronic El Niño", and governments blew billions of dollars attempting to rectify the problem.

Some say that this money was well spent, because as the clock chimed midnight planes failed to fall out of the sky and electronically controlled sewage plants failed to explode. True, 150 slot machines at a Delaware racetrack stopped working, and a few versions of Microsoft Excel had trouble with leap-year calculations. But in laid-back countries like Italy, where officials had shrugged their shoulders and assumed everything would be OK, nothing untoward happened. Suddenly, the media were labelling the fuelling of the Y2K panic as the "hoax of the century", despite the fact that they were largely responsible for it.

Putting on a Velcro suit and hurling yourself at a Velcro wall

Many applications of Velcro would have been fizzing around the mind of Swiss engineer George de Mestral when he first came up with the hook-and-loop idea in the late 1940s, but it's unlikely that one of those would have been to create amusement by suspending people a couple of metres above the ground on a sticky wall. He would no doubt have been delighted when NASA started using the material for serious purposes on space missions, even if the clothing industry was a bit slow on the uptake – but it wasn't until David Letterman stuck himself to a wall using Velcro during a live broadcast in February 1984 that the seeds of a quite different money-making idea were first sewn in the minds of wacky entrepreneurs.

The "sport" of Velcro jumping first took hold in New Zealand, but by the 1990s Americans were eager to run a few metres wearing a Velcro suit, jump off a small trampoline, and slam into a cushioned wall also covered in Velcro. Fairly free of danger (as long as the suit consists of hooks and the wall consists of loops or vice versa), it became a standard fairground attraction along with bucking broncos and bouncy castles – but there was never much of an adrenalin rush, and once you were stuck, all that there was left to do was peel yourself off and do it again. "Absolute madness", is how a British company still offering Velcro wall hire describes it, and that's pretty near the mark.

Making alcohol vastly more palatable to kids

Over the centuries, there's one thing that has remained a barrier to children curious about getting drunk, and that's the fact that children find alcohol, in the main, pretty unpalatable. Adults learn to adore its various characteristics because of the wonderful side effect of blotting out reality for three or four hours but, on the whole – and certainly to the novice drinker – beer tastes metallic and insipid, wine tastes rough and acidic, and spirits seem to strip the flesh from your oesophagus. Those who couldn't bear the taste would create saccharine concoctions such as Southern Comfort and lemonade, Malibu and pineapple or Amaretto and cola, but it wasn't until the appearance of alcopops in the early 1990s that people with unschooled palates could easily down huge quantities of alcohol and get completely legless without grimacing.

Bacardi Breezers blazed the trail, with their lip-smacking but undeniably alcoholic rum 'n' fruit mixtures, to be followed by such sugary creations as Two Dogs lemonade, and various varieties of Hooch. While the companies involved may well have claimed to be broadening the choice for consumers, their most immediate effect was to inebriate people who had previously not been that interested in drinking. As one writer put it, alcopops were a "fizzy drink which allows alcohol to pass into the bloodstream while bypassing the taste buds." Governments eventually made concerted efforts to slap taxes on them – which did lessen their consumption, but could never succeed entirely in putting much of a dent in the human need to get legless every so often.

Imagining that Girl Power would change society

Times have undoubtedly moved on from the state-supported wife beating of the 1500s (see p.52) but, women still earn less money than men for doing the same work, still experience sexual harassment, and still encounter career glass ceilings. In the 1990s, the "third wave" of feminism was doing its utmost to battle these continuing injustices – but the decade wasn't defined by third-wave feminism; it was defined by Girl Power. The 1990s global phenomenon of five-piece pop act the Spice Girls brought the phrase to the attention of everyone who wasn't living a hermit-like existence – but it didn't so much galvanize a women's movement as encourage ten-year-old girls to dress up in emulation of their favourite Spice Girl archetype, be it Sporty, Scary or Posh.

Which, of course, isn't in itself a bad thing. But while cultural commentators worked themselves up into a lather over this pseudo-feminism that seemed to be promoting gender equality in the young, the Spice Girls were shifting millions of records, bought by a newly mobilized demographic previously more interested in male pop stars. As a result, the legacy of Girl Power was a tidy pay packet for those who'd been involved in creating it, and a slew of unsuccessful copycat acts. In the meantime, the real battle of equality is still being fought – by people far less glamorous and wealthy.

Getting Celtic or Japanese symbols tattooed on your back

Getting tattooed isn't a pain-free experience, and for many years tattoos were badges of honour amongst slightly scary men who hung out in slightly scary pubs, recounting brutal anecdotes of fist-fights that would invariably end "and you should have seen the other guy." They would have their girlfriends' names permanently emblazoned on their forearms, unaware that this show of loyalty was unlikely to keep her in the relationship if he ended up serving an eight-year stretch for grievous bodily harm. But largely driven by high-profile celebrities such as Johnny Depp and David Beckham who made it cool to have dye injected into the dermis, the masses followed suit with millions of ill-advised tattoos which continue to embarrass their owners to this day.

While men frequently made the simple error of believing that they would love Linkin Park or the Manic Street Preachers in perpetuity, women were keener to adopt words such as "Strength" or "Peace", but using Celtic symbols, or Japanese or Sanskrit characters, to make these statements seem more exotic and profound. Of course, the translations were rarely checked over with qualified language experts, and as a result thousands of women are walking around with "Engine Oil" or "Bilberry" emblazoned on their lower back by mistake. The rapidity with which lower-back tats became unfashionable as everyone rushed to get them done (nearly forty percent of under-40s in the US have a tattoo) saw them become known as "tramp stamps". And worse still, you couldn't remove your tramp stamp without further pain and additional expense.

Wearing fashionable shoes that didn't ruin your feet

When we've already mentioned such crimes against chiropody as stilettos and platforms (see p.68) it seems a shame not to mention footwear that was good for your feet and provided more than adequate ankle-support. But the utilitarian aesthetic of Doc Marten boots seemed unlikely to ever make them fashionable; in the decade following their invention in 1947, eighty percent of sales were to German women over the age of forty. Even their adoption by post-punk counterculture in the UK and USA wasn't enough to give them mass-market appeal.

But the 1990s saw them become so popular that the people who had worn them to appear different suddenly had to jettison them, as hordes of pre-teenage girls snapped up new ranges of cutesy multicoloured DMs. This trend was mirrored by the newly found popularity of guitar music that had previously been bought only by a handful of floppy-fringed boys with emotional issues; suddenly everyone was listening to Nirvana, and traipsing around town in footwear whose soles were heat resistant to 80° C and provided superb protection

against dangerous acids. (Not usually a problem in shopping centres.)
A dedicated Doc Martens store opened in London's Covent Garden
at the height of the boot's popularity, but in 2003 all production ceased
in the UK as boys switched to ludicrously overpriced trainers, and girls
abandoned comfortable if hefty shoes for daintier footwear that seemed
designed to cut painfully into their heels.

Imagining that a jar of pesto will transform your culinary abilities

Boiling up some pasta and covering it in a heated-up jar of ready-made
tomato sauce to create a ridiculously quick meal was a lifeline for
hard-working folk in the 1980s who a) were continually pushed for time,
and b) couldn't cook to save their lives. But the introduction of pesto
onto the supermarket shelves was a further revelation, as pasta with
pesto actually requires less work than pasta with sauce (because the
pesto doesn't require heating up). And for a few short years, the meal
managed to combine ridiculous simplicity with an incredibly thin
veneer of sophistication.

Citizens of Genoa would probably shrink back in horror at a jar of
mass-produced pesto sauce, but we truly believed that we were eating
authentic Italian food, and that chucking a tablespoon of the stuff on
top of some overcooked rigatoni actually marked us out as talented
cooks. Student boys attempted to impress student girls by serving up
pasta with pesto, perhaps with a bit of extra grated parmesan cheese,
as their *pièce de résistance*. But it didn't take long for the pesto flourish
to fail in its attempt at seduction. Your guest quickly realized that the
cooking process was less involved than preparing a ham sandwich, and
in many ways not nearly as appetizing. Pesto would henceforth remain
in the cupboard for emergencies only – and if you wanted to impress,
you'd definitely have to get more than one pan out of the cupboard.

Sudoku puzzling and Viagra guzzling: The 2000s

10

We're barely emerging from the first decade of the twenty-first century, so it's hard to be objective about our recent behaviour. We're still wild about Harry Potter, but it's hard to know whether future generations will look back and wonder why we fussed over a fictional boy-wizard. The Ugg boot – a piece of footwear that women would have spurned in the mid-1980s – may well have returned to being a fashion faux pas by the time this book is published, but it's hard to know for sure. But other new traits are probably with us for good – say, a couple having their mobile phones sitting next to their plates while eating in a restaurant, what with the telecommunications boom showing no signs of slowing, and humans showing an inexhaustible need to stay in contact with everyone they know at all times.

More serious issues were also occupying our minds, and with good reason: the events of September 11, 2001 left us all wondering whether our lives would be similarly cut short by terrorist martyrs seeking eternal pleasure in the company of 72 virgins, while the melting of the polar ice caps and increasing frequency of freak weather events finally woke us up to the idea that global warming might not be such a far-fetched notion after all. But that didn't stop us attaching a singing fish to our wall. Speaking of which…

Attaching a singing fish to your wall

An entertainer who only has one string to his bow – say, a tap dancer who only knows the moves to "Putting On The Ritz", or a magician who can only make digital watches disappear – will quickly find their limited skills adversely affecting their careers. An act that might initially seem impressive and diverting will quickly become monotonous, repetitive and irritating – which is exactly the experience suffered by anyone who owned a Big Mouth Billy Bass. If there was ever something comical about a mechanical, rubbery fish singing "Don't Worry, Be Happy", said humour had a brutally short lifespan and has long since been forgotten by those who experienced it. But the fish couldn't be taken back to the shop because, despite being profoundly annoying, it did exactly what it was supposed to do.

It made its first appearance in niche sports stores in the USA in April 2000, and was soon selling in huge quantities to people who had never previously considered attaching a fish to their wall, let alone one whose vocal repertoire extended to one Bobby McFerrin number. But this was not a gift that kept on giving, and by the end of the year some were changing hands on eBay for under a dollar, while others failed to change hands at all. Dr Robert Thompson, professor of media and pop culture at Syracuse University, described Billy as "off the scale in terms of taste". If only we'd consulted such a doctor before making the mistake of buying one.

Boosting one's sexual potency with drugs acquired on the Internet

There's a reason that all drugs can't be bought off the supermarket shelf and that a doctor's permission is needed to get hold of them. It's not because the doctor is a killjoy; it's just that untrammelled drug free-for-alls aren't a particularly good idea – not least because stupid people might decide that the more medicine they take, the more beneficial the effect, and start gulping them as if they were breath fresheners.

But the Internet started to make prescriptions passé. Following the marketing of Viagra in the mid 1990s and its approval for use to treat erectile dysfunction in 1998, men were faced with the problem of having to admit that they had erectile dysfunction in order to benefit from the new treatment. And being proud, slightly vain characters, they didn't want to confess this to anyone other than a stranger operating a dodgy drug-selling website on the other side of the world. This had two effects: thousands of under-the-counter drugs winging their way across the globe in plain brown packets, and a massive proliferation of junk email. Of the millions of such emails, it only required a tiny percentage to yield orders – and even now, scarcely a day goes by without someone calling themselves something like Hamstring C Semifinalist sending us a note urging us to extend our manhood. Whether we have a manhood or not.

Attempting to rid the body of "toxins"

Here's some health advice included with this book at no extra cost: don't drink quite as much alcohol; cut back on processed food; eat more fruit and vegetables; don't spend all your free time slobbing on a sofa and working your way through successive boxes of chocolates. This is basic common sense, of course – but these rules, tarted up with jargon and repackaged in a white coat, thick-rimmed spectacles and a clipboard, were suddenly flying off the shelves in the early 2000s in the form of a range of so-called "detox" books that promised to help you "expel toxins". With svelte celebrities lending their wholehearted support, a huge industry quickly grew up around detox diet plans, despite the absence of scientific evidence that they detoxified you in any way.

It might seem churlish to complain about any movement that promotes healthy living, even if that advice essentially boiled down to "be more healthy", but there were extensions of the detox movement that weren't quite so benign; such as the dangerous suggestion that "water fasting" was beneficial. Ranges of detox products such as teas were widely sold, and at the height of the craze, credulous health-freaks would have bought microwavable sausages if they had the word "Detox" emblazoned on them. Soon, scientists were speaking up and pointing out that the body detoxifies itself perfectly well already, thank you, and reaffirming what we all knew, deep down: there's no magic solution to becoming healthier. You've just got to cut back on the burgers and booze.

Passing the time with a Sudoku puzzle

For some people, puzzles are a fearsome test of the human mind that is to be relished. Others aren't so keen on the mental battle, but enjoy the familiarity and gentle routine of an easy puzzle in the same way that they might enjoy mowing the lawn. The brilliant simplicity of Sudoku ticked both those boxes; when they first appeared in newspapers in 2004, hardcore cryptic crossword fans were as attracted to the form as those who preferred Spot The Difference. The idea of Sudoku is to fit the numbers 1 to 9 into a grid of 81 squares, without the numbers repeating in rows, columns, or clusters of nine (see puzzle, opposite) – but crucially there was no maths involved, a fact trumpeted by newspaper editors who'd print "no maths involved!" next to the grid in the hope that people would have a go. And have a go they did.

The chap who is thought to have invented the puzzle back in 1979, Howard Garns, died long before the craze took hold, and he would have

			3		8	5		
4							7	
			6	7	4	2		
	4	9					3	2
	1		4	2	7		6	
2	6					4	8	
		4	5	3	9			
	7							9
		3	7		2			

been surprised at the way the twenty-first-century media exploited Sudoku for all it was worth. Within a couple of years it had spawned TV shows, dozens of books and magazines, songs, electronic versions, a world championship and a three-dimension Rubik-a-like (see p.156). But what the puzzle didn't have going for it was variety, and despite attempts to inject new life into the old format (Super Sudoku, Hyper Sudoku, Killer Sudoku) it failed to stop people suffering from Sudoku overload, Sudoku boredom and, ultimately, Sudoku intolerance.

Trying to find a casual acquaintance on Friendster.com

It's not many years since "social networking" was a phrase that might be used solely by marketing executives wearing brightly coloured spectacles and standing in front of a flipchart full of similarly irritating buzzwords. But it has come to mean something beyond a mere Internet fad; its basic premise of "keeping you in touch with your friends" underlies almost every successful online venture, and the vast majority of unsuccessful ones, too. We've never been more in touch with our friends – indeed, it's scarcely possible to be out of touch with them. But for the Western world, the website that first put the idea into practice – Friendster.com – is now a virtual ghost town, a space where friends could certainly keep in touch with each other had they not departed en masse to the place where the real party is (supposedly) happening.

An investor in Friendster.com revealed in 2006 that the site's founder, Jonathan Abrams, created it as a "way to surf through friends' address books for good-looking girls" – and it initially succeeded magnificently: in 2003 people flocked to look at flattering pictures of friends of their friends, and Google soon offered Abrams thirty million dollars for the site. Abrams declined, figuring that the site would go from strength to strength. But while it continues to be popular in Asia, people in Europe and America have lost interest; there wasn't much intrinsically wrong with the website (after all, it ended up being superseded by MySpace, a far uglier offering) but, like a cool nightclub that suddenly and inexplicably falls out of favour, no one went there anymore. After connecting with your friends, there was nothing to do except go and connect with your friends somewhere else.

Going to work on a small, foot-powered aluminium scooter

The scooter takes its place alongside the tricycle as the first personal transportation devices for children, allowing them to propel themselves across playgrounds towards other children who then squeal and run out of the way. But for a two-year period, the foot-propelled scooter, in a miniature, fold-up form, would be used by grown adults to whizz around the City of London, Manhattan, and any number of regional airports – transforming these areas into playgrounds full of people in suits who were old enough to know better.

The micro-scooter was invented by a former Swiss banker named Wim Ouboter, whose life-long interest in scooters was borne out of the fact that his sister had one leg 25cm shorter than the other. At the peak of its popularity it was being described as a "travel essential", and picked up celebrity endorsements from the likes of Kylie Minogue and Robbie Williams. But the fad wasn't without its problems; during one boom period in the USA in May 2001, hospitals treated more than four thousand accidents in a month-long period, and in the UK the Royal Society for the Prevention of Accidents described the micro-scooter as being more dangerous than inline skating (see p.182). It may have looked sufficiently like a toy for helmet-wearing to seem pointless, but it could nip along at 25mph and was perfectly capable of propelling you over the handlebars. Today, the micro-scooter has transformed from being "a great idea" to being "slightly embarrassing".

Sporting an unpleasant-looking plastic leisure shoe

The popularity of the platform shoe (see p.68) showed that we can feel affection for unpleasant-looking footwear under certain precise cultural conditions, but no one would have placed any bets on love ever being shown towards a brightly coloured plastic clog. But during 2006 people suddenly began to sport Crocs, which had been aimed originally at boating enthusiasts and were made out of rubbery material known as "croslite". They were quickly branded as a fashion disaster, but the company behind Crocs hit back – not by denying it, but by running advertising campaigns with the strapline "ugly is beautiful". And by

making a virtue out of the fact that they looked pretty unpleasant, they started to cultivate a motley crew of admirers, including Al Pacino, George W Bush, and a whole heap of roadies who suddenly didn't have to take any socks on tour.

So they survived being criticized as hideous – but then they were attacked for a quite unexpected reason: health and safety. Despite having been certified by the US Ergonomics Council and described by more than one happy customer as "comfortable", they were suddenly accused of all manner of evils, from causing a build-up of static electricity to dragging children into escalator mechanisms. Regardless of whether the accusations had any sound basis, sales began to slump during 2008 – and the lack of activity today on both ihatecrocs.com and crocfans.com would indicate that the majority of people no longer care one way or the other about them.

Dipping a marshmallow into a chocolate fountain

As if we hadn't learned our lesson from the rapid rise and fall of the fondue set (see p.139), we briefly dug in our pockets in the middle of the decade to hire chocolate fountains for parties: a waterfall of smooth, melted chocolate into which you could stick strawberries, pineapple chunks, biscuits, cakes, in fact anything that tasted good when covered in melted chocolate – which, let's face it, is pretty much everything. "It turns every adult into a child," said one enthusiastic entrepreneur, failing to add that it turns every adult into a 200 lb child with rotten teeth. Because if there's one thing that doesn't help you keep tabs on your calorie intake, it's free-for-all dipping into a virtually inexhaustible supply of chocolate.

As with the fondue, there was also the potential of the "double-dip" transforming the beautiful chocolate fountain into a cascading pillar of germs and disease, which meant that eagle-eyed fountain police had to be on standby. There was also the issue of waste – not just the fact that you were powering up a device to pointlessly pump liquid chocolate around a circuit for four hours, but that when you were finished, some 10lb of semi-melted chocolate would remain adhering to the interior of the machine. Which was probably more than everyone at the party managed to consume over the course of the entire evening.

Driving a colossal sports utility vehicle to drop the kids off at school

Sometimes, bigger is better. An extra bedroom in your home can be useful, a grand piano sounds better than a honky tonk, and you get more of a thrill from a rollercoaster than a swing. But sometimes huge isn't so good. Brick-like mobile phones. Malignant tumours. And huge cars which are only used for casually zipping about town.

SUVs are often advertised as being all-terrain vehicles, perfect for embarking on a desert trek in Nambia, or exploring mountainous

Ways in which we have danced that would now look somewhat embarrassing

"Dance like nobody's watching," said Mark Twain – although if he'd lived longer than 1910 and had experienced some of the unpleasant free-form shapes that we have thrown in the name of dance from the jazz era through to the present day, he may have revised his advice to something like: "Dance like your father is watching, because there's no sense in making a fool of yourself." Of course, there have been people who can't dance for as long as there have been people who can, but it took the twentieth century to really bring all that arrhythmia out of the woodwork. Before then, dancing in Western culture tended to follow fairly rigid rules about what can and can't be done, and this resulted in a rather dignified spectacle, if slightly stilted and unenjoyable to participate in. There was the odd exception: for instance, the epidemic of dancing mania that gripped Europe for periods between the fourteenth and eighteenth centuries that involved flailing around as if possessed by Satan until you foamed at the mouth and dropped dead from sheer exhaustion. But among the cultured classes, a stately gavotte or minuet was more the order of the day.

All hell was let loose, however, at the point where we decided that it didn't really matter how we danced as long as we enjoyed ourselves. The emergence of dances like the Charleston in the 1920s and the Twist in the late 1950s were notable for a) the steps (such as they were) being incredibly easy to remember, b) not really

involving anyone else, so you were unlikely to put your partner off if you were rubbish, and c) being considered provocative by those who'd appointed themselves the moral guardians of that particular generation. Dance has never been solely responsible for any decline in moral standards, but some of the monsters we've created over the past century could certainly be classed as inadvisable, verging on inexplicable.

Take the conga. It started life perfectly innocently: a march that took place during Latin American carnivals where a line of people would gaily shuffle along in time to the music and kick just before the fourth beat in a syncopated, slightly exotic way. It grew in popularity in the USA from the 1930s onwards, but by the time the 1980s hoved into view it had lost any sophistication and was more about a colossal snake of boozed-up people desperately hanging onto the shirts of the person in front while clumsily circling the party venue for no particular reason. Other notable examples of this genre – dances that are less about dance than, er, music and movement – include the compulsion British people have to sit on the floor and pretend to be part of a rowing team whenever "Oops Upside Your Head" by the Gap Band starts playing, and, of course, the unedifying spectacle that suddenly manifests itself in front of a stage containing men with guitars and leather-studded belts: it might well be called "moshing", but it's really about everyone pushing everyone else while trying not to fall over.

Some dances are less about social bonding and more about showing off. When these are attempted by someone with grace, elegance and poise, they can just about work, but it's disastrous when the rest of us have a go. The limbo dance may well have its own cultural significance in Trinidad, but when Western tourists try, well, it's just fat people crawling under a stick. Breakdancing can be a thrilling spectacle, but few of us can spin on our heads at a wedding reception and get away with it. Madonna can "vogue" spectacularly, and Michael Jackson can undoubtedly simulate the movement of a robot, but most of the rest of us look like someone with a horrible combination of attention deficit disorder and haemorrhoids. There was less chance of embarrassing oneself in the days when dances came with official guidance, but we can at least hang on to one, small crumb of comfort: we almost certainly have more fun dancing exactly how we like.

regions of Chile. And so the criticism they attracted was often based on the fact that these huge vehicles were being required to tackle nothing more tricky than a mini-roundabout at the top of a suburban cul-de-sac: they were simply the wrong vehicle for the wrong job. But many SUVs don't come with the four-wheel drive that makes them suitable for off-roading, and would be as unsuitable for the jungle as a double-decker bus. So actually, they were just oversized cars. Cars that were statistically shown to be involved in more accidents, posed a greater risk to other road users than smaller cars, and guzzled about four times as much petrol. It wasn't long before the backlash started from ecologists, road safety experts, people who resented ostentatious displays of wealth, and, finally, politicians (when they realized that there might be a few votes in it). Sales in the UK declined as people realized that their status symbols were becoming stupidity symbols – although many still soldier on, keen to transport their shopping home in a roomy, three-ton air-conditioned box on wheels.

But surely these can't last, either?
The future

11

In moments when you're feeling particularly world-weary, you could probably make a list a couple of miles long of all the stuff you'd hope would quickly fade away into obscurity. Wet-look leggings. Vitamin water. Grubby bed and breakfasts that advertise themselves as "boutique hotels". And then there are the things that might have served you quite well and brought some comfort, or entertainment, but you have a nagging feeling that they might be destined for oblivion. Like newspapers. Or capitalism. Here are a few things that our children's children's children might look back at in wonder, awe or a sliver of contempt.

Paying ridiculously small amounts of money for sweatshop-produced clothing

You can buy a pair of trousers these days for less than the cost of a packet of cigarettes. By the time you've deducted shop worker's wages, storage and transportation you can imagine that the people employed in Far Eastern sweatshops might even be paying for the privilege of knocking up all that ill-fitting sportswear. Of course, we don't complain about the price – mainly because we're so far removed from the production process that we probably imagine the clothes are assembling themselves by magic. As the world economy rebalances, brace yourself for the return of kindly British tailors with a tape measure around the neck and the urge to measure your inside leg.

Teaching the theory of Intelligent Design in schools

Charles Darwin didn't know everything, but that doesn't mean Charles Darwin knew nothing. His theory of evolution was compelling enough for it to be accepted by the scientific community, but it never sat very squarely with the fundamental religious view that the universe was put together by some kind of Otherworldly Being. Hence Intelligent Design, a pseudo-scientific way of allowing creationism to be taught in schools; teachers actually stand in front of a class and tell them that the things scientists haven't managed to get to the bottom of are best explained by magic. Not the best way to educate the next generation of scientists.

Wearing one's trousers so one's underpants are showing

It's called "sagging", it allows men to display their underwear to the general public, and it's seen as utterly inexplicable by virtually everyone over the age of 35. It stemmed from hip-hop fashion, which in turn (supposedly) stemmed from the banning of belts in prison, which meant that everyone was perpetually pulling up their trousers or just allowing the waist band to descend to somewhere around the mid-thigh – a place it was never designed to loiter. Fortunately, the next generation seems to be rebelling; more than one child has been heard to complain, "Daddy, I can see your pants."

Becoming obsessed with minute details of the lives of minor celebrities

We invest so much time and effort in storing and recalling the relationship history of some bloke off the telly, including exactly what he has done, where he did it, when he did it and to whom he did it, that it's a wonder we can even remember our PIN or where we left our car keys. The media outlets which provide this information regularly point out that this tittle-tattle is only what people want to read, that they're only catering for demand rather than setting the news agenda. They're probably right. But perhaps, at some point, we'll realize how badly we've been misusing our brains, and devote them to more useful tasks such as solving the Palestinian question instead.

Expressing oneself online with a strict limit of 160 characters

The length of the humble text message was established as 160 characters back in 1985 when the technology was in its infancy. But with the rise of websites such as Facebook and Twitter – which were designed to work in tandem with mobile phones – this limit has become the standard length for communicating one's thoughts, and if you go over the limit, you're brutally cut short. This restriction has severely impeded human communication, forcing us to say things to each other like "i luk lyke i jst cme bk from a party nt getin ready 4 1 lol cnt wait."

Trying to cut rates of teenage pregnancy by advocating abstinence

The drive to have sex and procreate is a pretty strong one. We're designed that way to ensure the survival of the species, and if it wasn't for niggling problems like sexually transmitted diseases and the fact that most of us are picky about our sexual partners, we'd be having sex constantly and indiscriminately. But a third of President George W Bush's HIV budget was directed towards abstinence programmes, in a futile attempt to battle the human impulse. Researchers found that such programmes had no effect on maintaining virginity, use of contraception, incidence of disease, number of pregnancies or number of partners. Whoops.

Becoming obsessed with watching television programmes featuring normal people doing nothing of interest

There was a time when TV entertainment consisted of reasonably talented people telling jokes, doing magic tricks or singing Frank Sinatra cover versions. But we got bored with that, and developed a fascination for seeing talentless cretins displaying their uselessness for hour upon hour of prime-time viewing in a series of reality shows. Perhaps the point of watching was just to reassure ourselves that we were comparatively intelligent and likeable, but we may as well have turned off the television and just stared at each other instead.

Using a mobile phone that tries to do everything but has a terrible battery life

Modern portable technology presents us with a simple trade-off: either use a simple device that doesn't allow you to play backgammon, engage in video chat with a distant relative, or film your cat coughing up hairballs, or go for the one that has all the bells and whistles but requires you to carry around a charger and regularly ask people where the nearest electrical socket is. Battery technology hasn't really caught up – and it's hard to imagine that it ever will; manufacturers will always pack in unwanted features and leave us carrying around a power-free lump of black plastic.

Paying upwards of £50 per month to not go to the gym

Early January sees the increase in gym memberships soaring as we promise ourselves a brand new start, a new era of fitness, health and doing what's best for our longevity. But by mid-January, that feeling has been replaced with one of resignation as snacks inevitably make their way from the kitchen into our mouths. We continue to pay the membership fees in the hope that our monthly bank statement will prick our consciences and force us out of the house and onto a treadmill. But it never does. So gyms thrive on guilt, while remaining largely empty.

Arranging delivery of organic fruit & vegetable boxes

There are many and various reasons for opting to buy organic vegetables over the homogenous, plastic-wrapped stuff you get in the supermarket. But when they're delivered, they often send you diving for a recipe book or shaking your head in despair. Because nothing hits harder at your reserves of culinary inspiration than the sight of four swedes and a turnip. It's better for the planet than buying a pineapple that's been flown several thousand miles, but pineapples are just more appetizing.

Owning so many DVDs of television series that you couldn't possibly have time to watch them before you die

We're swamped by media. In bygone times, it used to be the case that if you missed a television series you'd have to wait until it was repeated before you could see it again. Video cassette recorders changed that, but DVDs present us with hour upon hour of footage on a single shiny disc, with umpteen additional features, extras and commentaries. And they're cheap, so they make good birthday presents. And they amass ominously on our shelves, doomed never to be watched – enough entertainment for several lifetimes, despite the fact that we only have, well, one.

Making your avatar dance in a virtual nightclub

There's a lot to be said for the Internet's ability to bring us together, but the rise of virtual worlds is curious; we assume control of an imaginary character, and get it to interact with other people's imaginary characters. *Second Life* is probably the strangest example, because it's not even a game; there's no point where you can actually say "Yes, I've succeeded." Its virtual nightclubs feature hundreds of avatars in outlandish clothing gyrating spectacularly on an imaginary dancefloor. But surely one life of being rejected by potential dance partners because of your lack of rhythm is enough?

Balancing a pair of shutter shades on your nose

Unless they have no lenses in whatsoever (see p.114) the whole point of spectacles is to make you see better. If you're short-sighted or long-sighted, they modify the focal length of your eye to bring objects into focus. If it's sunny, you wear sunglasses to reduce the glare and stop you squinting like a breakdown recovery engineer caught in headlights. Shutter shades, however, are notable for having a series of horizontal bars across the frames, making you feel like (and look like) you're peering through Venetian blinds. Kanye West is largely responsible for their popularity, and he should be ashamed of himself.

Wearing flip-flops when you're walking around a town or city in the summer

Beachwear rarely translates well to the high street. Few of us would parade around town in a bikini, swimming trunks or a sombrero. But the flip-flop – a slab of plastic loosely attached to your foot by a much flimsier strip of plastic – has recently become acceptable summer footwear for both men and women. Your feet get filthy, it's impossible to move at anything greater than a leisurely stroll, people accidentally step on them and send you crashing head-first through ticket barriers, and – perhaps most importantly – virtually everyone's feet look hideous.

Placing all our faith and trust in machines to make important things work properly

"Sorry, the computer isn't working", comes the reply when you call your bank, or your electricity supplier, or the local council, or your online grocery store, or your boss, or even your spouse: "I can't tell you whether we're free on the twentieth, darling, because I can't seem to connect to our online calendar." We've become so beholden to technology that we experience minor panic attacks when we realize we've left our mobile phone at home, and become irritable if we can't resolve a dispute in the pub about the cast of *Die Hard* 2 because the landlord has forgotten the wi-fi password for his router. What have we become?

Picture credits

Inside front cover, Geoff Dann © Dorling Kindersley; 8–9, Jorgen Angel/Redferns/Getty Images; 11, © Dorling Kindersley; 12, © Dorling Kindersley; 14, © Dorling Kindersley; 15, © Dorling Kindersley; 17, © Dorling Kindersley; 21, Andrew Clare; 22, Elliot Elam; 27, Elliot Elam; 29, © Dorling Kindersley; 33, © Dorling Kindersley; 34, © Dorling Kindersley; 36 © Rough Guides Dorling Kindersley; 38, Elliot Elam; 40, © Dorling Kindersley; 43, © Dorling Kindersley; 47, © Dorling Kindersley; 48, Elliot Elam; 54, © Dorling Kindersley; 55, © Dorling Kindersley; 56, © Dorling Kindersley; 58, Elliot Elam; 61, Elliot Elam; 63, © Dorling Kindersley; 65, © Dorling Kindersley; 67, © Dorling Kindersley; 70, © Dorling Kindersley; 72, © Dorling Kindersley; 74, © Dorling Kindersley; 77, © Dorling Kindersley; 81, Elliott Elam; 82, Elliot Elam; 84, © Dorling Kindersley; 85, © Dorling Kindersley; 88, © Dorling Kindersley; 89, © Dorling Kindersley; 92, © Dorling Kindersley; 93, © Dorling Kindersley; 95, © Dorling Kindersley; 99, © Dorling Kindersley; 100, Elliot Elam; 104, © Dorling Kindersley; 106, Elliot Elam; 110, © Dorling Kindersley; 112, squacco, flickr.com/photos/squeakywheel/488494653 Creative Commons Attribution-Share Alike 2.0 Generic; 113, © Dorling Kindersley; 116, © Dorling Kindersley; 118, © Dorling Kindersley; 121, Elliot Elam; 123, © Dorling Kindersley; 125, © Dorling Kindersley; 127, Elliot Elam; 130, © Dorling Kindersley; 133, © Dorling Kindersley; 134, © Dorling Kindersley; 137, aprillynn77, flickr.com/photos/aprillynn77/28864027, Creative Commons Attribution 2.0 Generic; 141, Elliot Elam; 143, flattop341, flickr.com/photos/flattop341/228342899, Creative Commons Attribution 2.0 Generic; 144, Elliot Elam; 148, © Dorling Kindersley; 149, Darwin Bell, flickr.com/photos/darwinbell/315051291, Creative Commons Attribution 2.0 Generic; 150, fimoculous, flickr.com/photos/fimoculous/3210330182, Creative Commons Attribution 2.0 Generic; 152, Elliot Elam; 153, © Dorling Kindersley; 155, jason_shipps, flickr.com/photos/jasonshipps/340169500, Creative Commons Attribution-Share Alike 2.0 Generic; 156, kirtpaph, flickr.com/photos/kirtaph/2919026200, Creative Commons Attribution 2.0 Generic; 159, © Dorling Kindersley; 161, cookipediachef, flickr.com/photos/cookipedia/3399540332, Creative Commons Attribution 2.0 Generic; 165, Elliot Elam; 166, © Dorling Kindersley; 169, © Dorling Kindersley; 171, © Dorling Kindersley; 172, © Dorling Kindersley; 176, Nagyman, flickr.com/photos/nagy/19705289, Creative Commons Attribution-Share Alike 2.0 Generic; 178, © Dorling Kindersley; 179, © Dorling Kindersley; 181, Elliot Elam; 183, Elliot Elam; 185, © Dorling Kindersley; 189, © Dorling Kindersley; 198, lizjones112, flickr.com/photos/lizjones/1094586860, Creative Commons Attribution 2.0 Generic; 200, Elliot Elam; 202, Salim Virji, flickr.com/photos/salim/1355763538, Creative Commons Attribution-Share Alike 2.0 Generic.

Index

A

Aborigines 123
Abrams, Jonathan 196
abseiling 125
abstinence 205
acacia tips 180
accidents 197, 202
acid house 172
acne 44
acting 52, 102
Adam Ant 175
adultery 16, 39, 69
advertising 95, 104, 118, 124, 128
aerobics 163
Aerosmith 176
Aëtius of Amida 180
afterlife, the 15, 105
AIDS 151
alchemy 64
alcohol 76, 87, 97, 126, 186
Alexander the Great 26
Alfred the Great 45
allec 24
almonds 28
alphabet, the 115
Amaretto 187
amber 108
American Medical Association 85
ammonia 107
Amsterdam 101
anaesthetics 22, 38
anal passage 16–17, 19

Angelow, Michael 145
animal rights 102
anthropomorphism 116
anti-biotics 35
archaeology 107
archery 44–45
architects 107, 113
aristocracy 33
Arithmetick 160
Ars moriendi 34
art 52, 162
Art Deco 107
asafoetida 19
Assize of Arms 45
Assize of Bread and Ale 49
Aston Villa 119
astrology 42
Athena 162
athletes 19, 154, 174
Atlantis 140
Attenborough, David 48
Augustus 25
auspices 27, 39
Australia 94, 123, 124

B

Baccara 147
Bach, J.S. 138
Baez, Joan 119
Baked Alaska 178
Baker's Baptism 50
baker's dozen 50
baldness 13, 80

balloons 92
Bandai 174
banking 153
banquets 26
Baraniuk, Daniel 97
barbers 37, 38, 54, 80
Barnum, P T 83
Bart Huges, Hugo 23
Bast 13
Bathing 21, 63
Bay City Rollers 8
beachwear 208
Beanie Babies 67, 179
beards 12
bears 141
beatniks 111
Beckham, David 188
beehive (hair style) 80
bees 141
begging 65
Behram, Thug 120
Benny Hill Show, The 17
Bentham, Jeremy 68
Berlin Wall 113
Berlioz, Hector 138
Bermuda Triangle 140
bestiaries 49, 53
bicycles 77
Big Mouth Billy Bass 192
bikinis 208
Biltong 24
binge drinking 87
birds 27
Birmingham City 119
birth certificate 121
Black And White Minstrel

Show, The 103
Black Death 32, 44, 51
blackface 103
Blackstone, Sir William 53
blacksmith 181
Blaine, David 97
Blanchard, Jean Pierre 92
bleach 60
blindness 102
blood 24, 26
bloodletting 54
Blue Peter 161
Blumenthal, Heston 133
Bocuse, Paul 158
boil-in-the-bag 133, 139
Bolivia 105
Bonaparte, Napoleon 71, 100
Bond, James 179
Bonnacon, the 49
Bono 95
books 50, 168, 193
boomerang 123
boredom 99, 102, 163, 195
Botox 72
Boulogne-sur-Mer 109
bouncy castles 186
Brady, Ian 120
brain, the 15, 23
Brand, Hennig 64
Braunhut, Harold von 116
brank 52
brass rubbing 73
Brazen Bull 100
bread 49, 92, 141

breakdancing 201
bribery 28
Brine shrimp 115
Britain 8, 36, 39, 46, 55, 66, 68, 73, 75, 117, 126, 130, 146, 158, 163
British Skin Foundation 60
Broadway 96
brown 122, 136
Brussels 130
Brutalism 113
Bubastis 13
bubbles 142
Buckaroo 67
bucking broncos 186
bungee jumping 178
Bunker, Chang and Eng 83
burglary 17
burial 14, 29
burns 118
Bush, George W 198, 206
Bwana Devil 128
Byers, Eben 87
Byham, Jackie 123
Byrds, The 114

C

Cabbage Patch dolls 162, 179
cakes 28
California 127
Cambridge 74

Index

cancer 31, 108
Canopic jars 15
capitalism 164, 203
caps 59
Carroll, Lewis 78
cars 59, 122, 166, 199
Carter, Howard 106
cassia 15
cats 12–14, 206
catwalk 110
CB radio 154
celebrities 121, 205
Chad 94
charioteers 19–20
charity 167
Charles, Jacques 93
Charles, Prince 146
charleston, the 200
Charlton, John P 98
chastity belt 39
chaudon sauce 33
chauvinism 168
chefs 133, 158, 177
chemistry 64, 107
chemotherapy 13, 167
Chicago 98
children 20, 28, 30, 67,
    72, 76, 78, 85, 109, 115,
    120, 136, 140, 142, 157,
    161, 162, 173, 186, 196,
    198, 205
Children's Comfort 85
chimney sweeps 141
Chinese whispers 49
chips 117, 154
chivalry 48
chocolate fountains 199
choking 157
cholera 35, 76
Choose Your Own
    Adventure 168
chopines 68
Christian Dior 170
Christianity 25
Christmas 25
Church, the 14, 73, 78
Churchill, Winston 78
cigarettes 108, 204
cinnamon 28

Citizens Band Radio 154
civilization 11
Civil Rights Movement
    118
Clackers 136
clarinet 57, 94
climate change 113
cloning 172
clothing 19, 24, 31, 59,
    89, 119, 126, 204
coal 107
Coca-Cola 142, 181
cockatrice, the 53
Cocker, Edward 160
codpiece 57
Cold War 91, 113, 132
colloquialisms 160
Cologne 44
comfrey 43
Commentaries of The
    Laws of England 53
communes 129
communism 164
community charge 177
compensation 45
computers 171, 184, 209
concrete 113
condoms 180
conga 201
Connect 4 139
Connecticut 148
conservatism 73, 111, 126
contraception 30, 180,
    206
convenience food 133
Convoy 154
cookery 33, 53, 117, 133,
    139, 158, 176
cooking oil 118
cornflakes 73
Coryate, Thomas 69
cosmetics 56, 60
counterculture 112, 119,
    129
Covent Garden 190
cramp 141
creationism 204
Crécy, Battle of 44
cremation 15

Crete 21
crinolette 90
crinoline 89
crockery 146
crocodile dung 180
crumhorn, the 57
crystal garden 107
cuckoldry 17
cummerbund 166
Curie, Marie 86
curry 133
Curry And Chips 147
curses 20, 50
Cyrene, North Africa 19

D

Dahl, Gary 142
Dallas 169
dance 96, 125, 157, 200,
    208
dandelions 140
danse macabre 34
Darwin, Charles 204
dates 28
de Mestral, George 186
Deacon, Joey 161
dead, the 14, 15, 16, 29
deadly nightshade 61
Dean, Christopher 62
death 34, 61, 67, 84, 85,
    87, 91, 100, 141, 174
death penalty 13
decomposition 15
Deely boppers 152
deep fat frying 117
deformity 67, 82, 86
Delaware 185
democracy 16, 46
dentistry 38, 55
deodorant 170
Depp, Johnny 188
depression 11, 13, 125, 126
depression gardens 107
designers 106
detox 193
dialysis 167

Diana, Princess 60, 172
Die Hard 2 209
diet 118, 194
disco 132, 151, 184
disease 19, 35, 87, 148,
    199
divining 39
DIY 136
Doc Marten boots 189
dogs 132
domestic violence 52,
    187
douching 181
Drake, Charlie 123
drill 22
drive-ins 122
Dr James' Soothing Syrup
    85
drowning 101, 141, 180
drugs 84, 130, 172, 193
    antipsychotic 23
    cannabis 85
    ecstasy 172
    LSD 125, 126
    psychedelic 119, 125,
    126, 129
drunkenness 87, 97, 146,
    186
Duncan Toys 128
DVDs 207
Dynasty 169

E

Easter eggs 132
eBay 175, 182, 192
economy 204
Edward III 45, 62
Edward VII 109
eggs 28, 167
Egypt 12–16, 60, 106, 180
8-track cartridges 10
Einstein, Albert 78
electric shock therapy 73
elephants 26, 103, 141,
    182
El Fisgón 94
Elizabeth I 58, 59, 62, 70

El Niño 185
email 41, 193
employees 25
endowment mortgages
    153
Enfield, Harry 160
English Channel 92
English Language 41, 115
English Statute of
    Artificers 66
engraving 20
enigmata 37
entrails 24
epaulettes 133
erasers 157
erectile dysfunction 193
Esperanto 109
Essex 173
Etch-A-Sketch 150
Ethiopia 151
etiquette 63, 139
European Convention on
    Human Rights 53
evolution, theory of 204
execution 28
executive toy 159
exercise 18, 163
Exeter Book, The 37
extinction 19
eyes 208
eyebrows 12, 61

F

Facebook 205
facelifts 131
factory farming 24
fake tanning 60
Fame 157
Family Fallout Shelter 112
famine 32
fans 88
farmers 46
farthingale, the 90
fashion 13, 57, 58, 60, 80,
    89, 107, 108, 114, 126,
    131, 152, 154, 165, 169,
    184, 189, 191, 204, 208

fat 24
Feast Of The Tail 16
feather cut 80
feet 209
femidom 181
feminism 126, 132, 187
Feralia 29
festivals 25, 62
feudal system 32
fibre optics 159
Field Book Of Wound Medicine 54
fighting 11, 140, 188
Fighting Fantasy 54, 168
film 122, 128
Finland 97
Finvenkismo 109
fire 93, 118
fireworks 107
fish 24
flagellation 32
flagpoles 96
Flashdance 158
flip-flops 208
flooring, laminate 135
Flores, Pedro 127
Florida 140
flower-children 129
flowers 107
flu 92
flute 57
Fonda, Jane 163
fondue 139, 199
food 19, 24, 26, 28, 29, 53, 55, 133, 139, 158, 176, 190
football 174
footwear 190, 191, 197, 209
Ford Zephyr 122
fortune-telling 28
four-wheel drive 202
France 103, 109, 158
freak shows 82
free love 129
Friendster.com 196
frost fair 62
funerals 14, 18, 86

G

Gall, Franz Joseph 74
gallantry 47
gambling 25
games 67, 79, 104, 117, 142
gamma rays 113
Gap Band, The 201
Garns, Howard 194
garum 24
gas 92
Gauls 22
gavotte 200
geeks 171
Geisslerlieder 32
Geldof, Bob 151
generosity 79
genitalia 18–19, 39, 57, 100
Genoa 190
geomancy 39
George II 70
Georgia, University of 145
Georgian era 41, 80
Germany 93, 124, 189
Gerson, Jean 43
gifts 25
gin 87, 142
Giorgio Beverly Hills 35, 64, 170
Girl Power 187
glam rock 184
glasses 114
glitter 184
Glitter, Gary 68, 133
global warming 192
gold 64
Goldeneye 179
goldfish 99
Google 196
Goths 24, 30
government 76, 87, 93, 97, 103, 164, 177, 185, 187
graffiti 94
Granby, Marquis of 160
graveyards 29

Great Depression, the 92, 97, 107
Greece 12, 17, 18–19, 21, 24, 26, 94, 100
greed 153
Greville, Fulke 120
Gulf War 172
gunpowder 27
gym 21, 207

H

hair 13, 80, 111
hallucination 125
Hamnett, Katherine 151
hanging 100
Hansburg, George 96
haruspex 28
Harvard 99
Harvey, William 55
Hasbro 139
haute cuisine 158
Hawaii 175
headaches 22
health 12, 86, 145, 193, 207
health and safety 25, 63, 93, 118, 198
Heb Sed 16
helium 93
henna 60
Henry VIII 57
herbs 19, 43
Herman's Hermits 125
hernia 141
heroin 85, 126
Hieorcles 40
Hieroglyphs 106
Hindenburg 94
Hindley, Myra 120
hip hop 94, 204
hippies 119
Hippocrates 22
HIV 206
hobbies 74
Hoffman, Albert 125
Hogarth, William 88
Hollandersky, Gilbert 102

Hollingshead, Richard 122
Holly, Buddy 172
honey 29, 55, 101, 180
Hooch 187
hot-air balloon 92
housing 75, 153
hula-hoop 124
human rights 102
humour 40
Hungary 97
hydrogen 93
hygiene 63

I

ibuprofen 22
ice 62
Iceland 97
Ice skating 147
Ice Storm, The 148
Illinois 86, 130
immigration 99
India 120
Industrial Revolution 71
inheritance 30
injury 45, 77, 96, 137
inline skating 96, 182, 197
insects 101
Intelligent Design 204
Internet 23, 150, 154, 159, 167, 177, 182, 193, 208
Iron Maiden 101
ITA 115
Italy 185
It Came From Outer Space 128
Ivan the Terrible 101
ivory 108

J

Jackson, Michael 32, 201
James I 70
James, Richard 104
Janov, Arthur 143
Japan 117
Jayne's Expectorant 85
Jazz 92

Jefferson Airplane 112
Jermajesty 121
Jews 44, 109
JFK 112
Joe Miller's Jests 41
Johnson, William 83
Jones, Tom 95
Jordan, Michael 176
Judas Cradle 101
Jump Jim Crow 102
jury system 36
justice 17

K

Kantner, Paul 112
karaoke 14
Kellogg, John Harvey 73
key parties 148
Kelly, Alvin "Shipwreck" 96
Kent, Clark 114
Kilroy, James 94
kitchenware 146
Kline, Kevin 148
knights 47
knitbone 43
Kum Ba Yah 118
KV62 106
Kynodesme 19

L

lactic acid 180
ladders 141
language 78, 89, 109
Lash Lure 61
Latin 18, 78
laundry 64
lava lamp 130
law 17–18, 21, 35, 45, 52, 62, 70, 87, 98, 154, 173, 177
lead 20, 61
League of Nations 109
leather 19
leeches 51
left-handedness 78

Index

leg warmers 157
Leigh, Mike 158
Lennon, John 144
lemon 180
leopard skin 14
leotard 163
lepers 44
Letterman, David 186
Lettuce 12
Lewis, Carl 18
libation pipe 29
Life Is Sweet 158
limbo dance 201
linen 16
Linkin Park 188
liquamen 24
Little Lord Fauntleroy 110
liver 28
lizard 180
lobotomy, frontal 23
London 62, 87, 100, 114, 190
Los Angeles 128
lotus flowers 106
Love Thy Neighbour 147
Lucian 25
luck 140
Luddites 72

M

mackerel 24
macramé 137
Madonna 61, 201
Mafia, the 98
magic 20, 204
magnetism 83
magpies 184
Magritte, René 162
Mainz 44
make-up 60
Malibu 187
Man and Baby (poster) 162
Mandela, Nelson 172
mandolin 139
Manic Street Preachers 188

Manilow, Barry 140
Manson, Marilyn 30
manticore, the 49
Marcel wave 80
marketing 89, 143
Marmite 24
Marne, First Battle of the 103
marriage 28
Marseille 22
marshmallow 199
Marxism 164
Massage belts 145
mass murderers 120
masturbation 39, 72
materialism 111
MB Games 139
McFerrin, Bobby 192
McGrath, Paul 119
media 205, 207
Medicamina Faciei Femineae 60
medicine 22–23, 54, 66, 84, 86, 193
Melbourne 123
mental illness 23
mercuric sulphide 61
mercurochrome 107
mercury 66
Mesmer, Franz 83
Mexico 94, 142
Miami Vice 165
miasmas 35
micro-scooter 197
Microsoft Excel 185
microwave 133
Middle East 39
military uniforms 103
milk 29
millennium bug 184
Milligan, Spike 147
mincemeat 55
mines 72
miniskirts 126
Minogue, Kylie 197
minuet 200
mobile phone 191, 205–206, 209
mock executions 101

monarchy 16, 146
money 153, 204
monks 37
monogamy 148
Montgolfier brothers 92
mood rings 135
Moors Murders 120
morality plays 42
morals 97
Morehead, Debbie 163
morphine 85
moshing 201
Mousetrap (game) 139
movies 92, 102
Mozart, W.A. 95
Mrs Winslow's Soothing Syrup 85
mullet 80
mummification 12, 15, 106
murder 16, 30, 45
mushrooms 141
music 52, 56, 95, 132, 134, 138, 148, 151
myrrh 15
MySpace 196
myths 53, 89

N

nagging 52
nails 149
Names 120
NASA 186
nasal strips 175
National Gallery 114
national press 99
Native Americans 78
NATO 155
natron 15
Nazis 109, 120
Neolithic era 22, 23
Nero 20
New Jersey 94
news 205
Newton's Cradle 159
New York 152, 170
New York (magazine) 184

New Zealand 121, 124, 186
Nightingale, Florence 35
9/11 192
Nirvana 189
noise 136
Norman conquest 120
Norse tales 37
Norway 97
nose 15, 174
nostalgia 122
nouvelle cuisine 158
nuclear family 129
nuclear war 112, 185
nudity 18, 129

O

obesity 154
O'Brien, Michael 145
odours 24–25, 35, 63, 157, 170
off-roading 202
office parties 139
offshore banking 177
oil crisis 132
Old Testament 120
Olympics 19, 123
omens 28
One Day Cough Cure 85
On Wounds Of The Head 23
Ono, Yoko 144
opera 108
opium 85
organic fruit 207
origami 137
Ouboter, Wim 197
Ouija board 105
Ovid 60
owls 137

P

Pacino, Al 198
packaging 132
paedophilia 134
palm wine 15

panacea 19
Parentalia 29
Paris 84, 92
Parker, Robert 135
parlour games 79
partner-swapping 148
parties 25, 26, 148
pasta 139, 190
patent 98, 130
patriotism 146
Peasants' Revolt 177
peasants 46
pederasty 21
pedestrians 182
Pelé 18
Pelusium, Battle of 13
Penfield, Bill 97
Penn & Teller 105
penny farthing 77, 96
Pepys, Samuel 100
perfume 64, 170
perpetual motion 159
Perry, Adam 162
Persecution 44
Persians 13, 26
pesto 190
Pet Rocks 142, 163, 173
pets 115
pewter 20
pharaohs 13, 16
Philadelphia 104
Philagrus 40
Phillip of Orange, Prince 23
Philogelos 40
Phoenicians 66
phonetics 115
phosphorus 65
photography 85
phrenology 75
physical fitness 16
picnicking 29
pig intestines 180
pigs 27
pilgrimages 32
Pill, the 181
pin art 159
pineapples 207
Pitman, Sir James 115

Index

placebo 18, 144
plague 34, 35, 73
planets 83
plaques 73
plaster 174
plastic 124, 133, 197, 207, 208
platform shoes 189
Pliny the Elder 180
poetry 12, 21, 148
pogo sticks 96
pogs 175
Poison (perfume) 170
Poland 94
polar ice caps 192
Polaroid 128
pole-sitters 97
police 173
police helmet 146
poll tax 177
pompadour 80
Pope, the 32, 69
population 21
portraiture 86, 146
postcards 98
potash 24
Potlatch 78
Potter, Harry 191
poverty 46
power 28
power-dressing 168
Power Rangers 176
prayer 140
prediction 27, 39, 74
pregnancy 205
Presley, Elvis 95, 138
priests 16
Primal scream therapy 143–144
prison 204
privacy 75, 122, 129
procreation 180, 205
Prohibition 98
promiscuity 148
Prostitutes 94
protest 177
psoriasis 44
psychology 101, 143, 144
psychotherapy 84, 125

public stunts 97
Puerto Rico 140
punishment 100
punk 80, 132, 189
Puritans 120
push-pin 68
puzzles 156, 194
puzzle mug 40
pyramids 101, 106

Q

Queen, the 33, 146
Quincy, Massachusetts 94

R

racism 103, 147
radioactivity 86
radishes 16
radium 86
rainbows 140
rape 17, 39, 43, 47
rational dress movement, the 90
raving 172
Reagan, Ronald 164
rebellion 126
recession 171
recorder 56
religion 14, 32, 105, 120, 204
remote control 12
Renaissance, the 51, 60
repetitive beats 173
repression 111
retro chic 130
revolution 46, 164
Reynolds, Joshua 135
Richard II 33
riddles 37
ring pulls 167
riot 87
Rite Of Spring 138
rituals 140
rivers 62
rivets 94

Roaring Twenties 92
Robuchon, Joël 133
rock music 138
rock'n'roll 95
Roe, Erica 146
Rollerblading 182
rollerskating 147
Romans 12, 17–19, 21, 24, 26, 27, 28, 29, 31, 39, 94, 180
Roosevelt, Franklin D 98
Rosarito Beach 142
ROSPA 197
royal family 110
Rubik's Cube 156
ruffs 58
rugby 146
rugs 135
Russia 97

S

sackbuts 57
sacrifice 28
sagging 204
sailors 109
St Mary's University, Minnesota 102
St Simeon Stylites the Elder 96
Sale Of Spirits Act 88
salt 107
sand 39
Sandoz Laboratories 125
sanitation 76
Santana 122
sardines 117
Satan 200
Saturnalia 25, 30
Saw, the 100
scaphism 101
scarabs 106
school 56, 115, 174, 204
scooters 196
Scotland 8
scrunchy 81
Sea-Monkeys 116
séances 105

seat belts 166
Second Life 208
security 50, 146
seduction 21
seeds 19
Seekers, The 119
Sem priests 14
sensory deprivation 101
serfs 46
Seth 14
sex 12, 20, 21, 39, 124, 126, 142, 148, 162, 180, 193, 205
Sex And The City 81
Sex Pistols, The 132
sexual harassment 187
sexually transmitted diseases 181, 206
shag-pile carpet 134
Shakespeare, William 41
shame 72
shaving 13
shell suits 154
ships 94
shoes 141, 189, 197
Crocs 197
platform 68, 131, 197
Short shorts 126
shoulder pads 168
shrine 13
shutter shades 208
Siamese twins 83
silphium 19, 20
silver 66
silver jubilee 146
Simpsons, The 172
Sinatra, Frank 206
singing 118
sitcoms 147
skateboarding 125
skull 22, 74
slavery 23, 25, 30, 71
slinky 104
smallpox 73
Smart Cars 117
Smokey And The Bandit 154
snacks 207
snoring 175

soap 24, 25
social class 46, 56, 88, 108
social networking 196
social status 19, 56, 68
SodaStream 142
soft drinks 142, 167
soldiers 39, 44, 47, 103
solitary confinement 101
sombrero 208
souls 12, 105
South Africa 117
South America 119
South East Asia 119
Southern Comfort 187
Spain 55
Spanish Inquisition 101
speakeasies 98
spectacles 61, 208
Spice Girls, the 52, 187
spiritualists 105
Spirograph 149
sports 18, 174
sports utility vehicle 199
sportswear 204
Spot The Difference 194
Sputnik 111
Sri Lanka 27
starvation 34, 174
state, the 164
stationery 157
status symbols 108
Statute of Caps 62
steamer 139
Stewart, Rod 80
stilettos 189
stoles 152
Strasbourg 44
Stravinsky, Igor 138
streaking 145
strigil 24
string art 149
Stubbes, Philip 59
students 99, 114, 145, 148, 190
suburbia 148, 202
Sudoku 194
sugar 55
suicide 30

215

Index

sumptuary laws 62
sunglasses 208
supermarkets 190, 207
superstition 86, 140, 180
surgery 37
SUVs 199
swans 33
Swanee River 102
sweatshops 204
swimming trunks 208
swing era 95
swingers 142
Switzerland 125
syphilis 67
Syracuse University 192

T

tabloid newspapers 152
Tagalog 127
Tamagotchi 173
tam-o'shanter 9
tartan 8, 132
tattoo 188
tax 75, 164, 177
teachers 204
Tears For Fears 144
Technicolor 128
technology 205, 206, 209
teenagers 8, 147, 152,
    160, 189, 205
teeth 55, 199
telephones 98
telephone boxes 117
telethons 178
television 103, 146, 161,
    206, 207
    breakfast 163

reality shows 99, 206
terrorism 31, 113, 132, 151,
    192
text messaging 205
Thames, River 62
Thatcher, Margaret 164
theatre 42
Théâtre des Champs-
    Élysées 138
thermotropic liquid
    crystal 135
Thompson, Dr Robert
    192
3D movies 128
tie-dying 119
Till Death Us Do Part 147
Tkaczuk, Józef 94
toenail clippings 129
togas 12
toilet-roll cover 158
toilet rolls 132
Tollund Man 107
Tom Thumb 83
tomato ketchup 24, 146
top hats 178
tortoises 173
tortoiseshell 108
torture 35, 100, 139
Torvill, Jayne 62
toxins 193
toys 128, 136, 156, 159,
    162, 174–175
tracksuits 154
trademark 128
trepanation 22
trial by combat 36
trial by ordeal 35, 69
tripping 119

trousers 204
    flared 131
trumpets 57
Tudor era 53, 66
Tupperware 124
Tutankhamen 106
Twain, Mark 200
twist, the 200
Twister 139
Twitter 205
Two Dogs lemonade 187

U

Ugg boot 191
UN Declaration of Human
    Rights 100
underwear 39, 204
United Nations 91
universe 204
uranium 87
urine 24, 64, 180
USA 61, 79, 97, 105, 107,
    110, 117, 124, 125, 130,
    145, 147, 160, 201
US Ergonomics Council
    198
US government 112, 126

V

Valley of the Kings 107
Vanuatu 178
Vaseline 156
vegetables 207
vegetarianism 129
Velcro 186

velocipede 77
Venetian blinds 208
Vermeer, Johannes 162
Viagra 193
Victoria, Queen 109
Victorian era 41, 60, 73,
    78, 86, 149
video games 168
video cassette recorders
    122, 207
Vienna 84
vinegar 61
virginity 43, 206
virtual worlds 208
Vlad the Impaler 101
vogueing 201
vomit 26
von Gersdorff, Hans 54

W

W & A Gilbey 142
Wales 177
Walker, Edward 130
Walkmen 183
war 27–28, 34, 47, 71,
    103, 111, 112, 120
    civil war 71
Warburg, Battle of 160
water 25, 76, 86, 107, 141
waterboarding 101
Waterloo, Battle of 103
Wayne's World 161
weapons 45, 123, 127
weasels 53, 180
weather 140, 192
Weaver, Sigourney 148
weregild 45

Wernick, Marvin 135
West, Kanye 208
whooping cough 141
wigs 13, 106
Wildlife and Countryside
    Act 33
Williams, Robbie 197
windows 75
wing collars 131
Winterhalter, Franz 110
witches 36, 69, 141
World Of Warcraft 176
World War I 91, 93, 103
World War II 101, 164
World Wide Web 171
writing 78

Y

yo-yos 127
youth culture 122, 124
Yugoslavia 172

Z

Zamenhof, Ludwik 109
Zappa, Frank 121
Zappa, Moon Unit 121
zeitgeist, the 9
Zeppelin 93
Ziegfeld Follies, The 96
zip 92
Zip the Pinhead 83
zombies 23
Zoroastrians 10
Zwarte Piet 103